WHEN
SURRENDER
WAS NOT
AN OPTION

WHEN
SURRENDER
WAS NOT
AN OPTION

by George G. Crawford
with James V. Lee

WHEN SURRENDER
WAS NOT AN OPTION

First Printing, 2001

ISBN 0-9663870-3-1

LCCN 2001 126665

Salado Press
P.O. Box 719
Salado, Texas 76571

Printed and bound in the United States of America.
Cover photo courtesy of San Diego Aerospace Museum.

DEDICATION

This story is dedicated to the memory of:
Captain Azorin, M.D., the senior French officer
of the Slave Labor Camp, for keeping me
alive during troubled times, and to Colonel
Spivey and to General Vanaman, for leadership
inspiring me to harass the enemy, yet survive.

CONTENTS

Photo Courtesy American Airpower Heritage Museum, Inc., Midland, TX

INTRODUCTION

When Surrender Was Not An Option is the dramatic World War II account of 2nd Lt. George G. Crawford's experience as a prisoner of war in Nazi Germany from the time his B-24 bomber was shot down until his liberation and return to the United States. It is a saga of men on the cutting edge of courage who did not just endure a long Nazi nightmare. Rather, in the best tradition of U. S. military duty, George and his fellow captives resisted and harassed the enemy in every way possible. By elaborate escape methods, they diverted thousands of German troops who otherwise would have been on the fighting front. Although his captors temporarily emaciated his body, they failed to extinguish his indomitable spirit, which serves as an example and inspiration to all Americans.

Jack W. Tarbutton
2nd Lieutenant, U.S. Army Air Corps
Pilot, B26 Bomber
12th Air Force
Nazi P.O.W. from October 1944 to April 1945
Stalag Luft III

Bombing of Monte Abbey Cassino Photo Courtesy Fred Riley

THE LAST MISSION

We had a rough mission that day bombing the Monte Abbey Cassino. Flak filled the sky, but for the first time the 456th Heavy Bombardment Group dropped all bombs at the same time the lead bombardier dropped his bombs. Saturation bombing.

Our Commanding Officer thought his bombardier could do no wrong. Of course, the C. O. was a little prejudiced, since his bombardier spent most of his time "sucking up." Personally, I thought the lead bombardier was blind in one eye and couldn't see out of the other. The Monte Abbey Cassino mission proved me right.

We had had a good briefing for the mission with excellent pictures of the target. The Abbey sat on top of a mountain with a river on one side and a railroad on the other. A large problem was the forest of flak guns around the Abbey that the Germans were using as a command post. We had a clear sky and good visibility, except for all the exploding shells.

Still, our lead bombardier couldn't find the target! We were getting all shot up as we followed the C.O.'s pet in a cloverleaf pattern around the Abbey until he could find the target. Finally, the blind man found the Abbey, and we plastered the target and returned to our home base looking like a bunch of cheese graters.

After landing at our base at Foggia, Italy, we learned that the German Command and all troops, except the anti-aircraft gun crews, had taken shelter in the caves, catacombs, and base-ments, thus not suffering any casualties from our bombing. When our ground troops went up the hill, they not only got shot up but were driven back a few miles.

Our planes were patched up that night, but the damage was so great that the flight crews got the next day off. After sleeping late and having breakfast in the mess tent, I went to the flight line to see how the repairs were going on our plane. We really had been lucky, as there wasn't too much damage, and only our flight engineer had earned a Purple Heart. I climbed into our plane to check out the bomb-release mechanism. Some of the planes in the 456th Group had bomb releases that malfunctioned or had bomb-bay doors that did not open wide enough.

Suddenly I found myself thinking of *For Whom the Bell Tolls* and Hemingway's description of the smell of death. The odor of our plane fit the description exactly. I looked for something dead or dying but found nothing, just that overwhelming, evil odor. I asked the ground crew if they smelled anything rotten, but I was the only complainer. I checked out the bombsight in the nose, and then I knew. I was certain that the odor was a warning that not all of us were coming back from our next mission.

The premonition grew stronger. What could I do about it? Was I going only one way next time? Was my wife going to be a widow? I didn't think that would happen, but I knew that not all of our crew would make it back the next day. I then reviewed the manual on emergency procedures and made certain that the release handle on the nose-wheel door operated smoothly and didn't hang up. That might be my exit in case of trouble.

What should I do? Should I tell the rest of the crew of my concern? I decided against that, as it might cause some of the crew to get nervous and really screw up. I did write my last letters to my wife and to my dad telling them how much I loved them. I also told my wife not to be a professional widow but to get married soon, because she was too good to go to waste. Then I ate an early dinner and went to sleep with my parachute as my pillow. I wanted to be certain it would be in good shape tomorrow.

After an early breakfast the next morning, we went in for our briefing. The mission looked pretty good—another raid on Vienna, Austria. Our raid there last week had been a long trip, but a real milk run. No fighters and no flak. Then the weatherman told us the target might be socked in. Lots of clouds. Our secondary target would be Klagenfurt, Austria, on the railroad marshaling yards that had never been hit before. That might be another milk run. Good news, but I knew better.

Then it was out to the flight line where our plane was gassed up and holding a full load of 500-pound G.P. bombs. Our four engines roared to life. All systems checked out okay, but I still smelled death all around me. Next, we taxied around on the steel mats that kept us from sinking into the Foggia swamp on our base. Suddenly, we ran off the mats and sank up to our wheel hubs into that awful muck.

I was delighted! We couldn't go on this damn mission! Our crew was safe from death or worse. Other planes had run off the mats before, and it always took at least a day to dig them out. There was no way we would be able to fly this mission. Quickly, the ground crew came out with a little tractor. I grinned. That little tractor couldn't get our heavy plane out of that muck. The tractor driver hooked onto the nose wheel, revved up his engine, and popped us right up and out of the mud and onto the mat. I couldn't believe it! This couldn't have happened, but it had. Now there was nothing to do but sweat.

We took off and headed for Split, Yugoslavia. I told Lt. Morris Turitz, the navigator, to wake me up if we ran into trouble or when we approached Vienna. Then, putting my head on my parachute, I went to sleep. No use worrying about the future now. Fate was, I knew, against us.

Turitz woke me up when we flew through the Brenner Pass as the Germans were shooting down on us with 88s from the mountaintops, but we didn't pick up any damage. As deputy lead for the entire 15th Air Force, we could see that, for a change, the weatherman was right. Vienna was socked in. We couldn't see the target. No target, no fighters, no flak. Maybe I was wrong about my premonition. I hoped so.

We took a new heading for Klagenfurt. I picked up the target in my bombsight, and then the lead plane aborted. Moving into the lead position, we picked up the target again and made our run. I announced, "Bombs away!" Then I heard a man's voice say, "Back, George!" I felt hands on my shoulders pulling me back violently, even though there was no one behind me. A chunk of flak came up through my bombsight, taking off the front of my oxygen mask and filling my face and eyes with small particles of airplane, bombsight, and flak. At first, I thought I was blind. Turning my head out of the wind, I blinked my eyes. What I saw made my eyes well in a hurry! Flames were shooting up the tunnel to our position in the nose. I grabbed a fire extinguisher and turned it on the flames, but the fire burned brighter. We had to get out! I opened the door on the nose turret, jerked out Sgt. Archie Rich, the gunner, and yelled for him to check his parachute. As I turned around, I saw Turitz jumping on the nose-wheel door. Since I knew from reading the escape manual that jumping on the door could jam it and trap us, I pulled him back and told him to put on his parachute. After obeying my own instructions, I pulled on the lever and gently pressed my foot on the door. It popped right off—just as the manual had said it would.

Turning, I looked at Rich and Turitz, gave them a "thumbs up," and bailed out. My uncle Seth, an aircraft engineer from way back, had advised me that if I ever had to bail out, not to pull the ripcord until I couldn't hear any engines so as to avoid getting tangled up with any planes. After all was quiet, I put my left arm in front of my face and pulled the ripcord with my right. I was falling with my back toward the ground. When my chest pack parachute opened, I did a violent back bend, injuring my neck and lower spine. I felt paralyzed, but peaceful.

Then all was quiet until I noticed a slight popping noise. I looked up at my parachute where the edges were fluttering, thinking that must be causing the popping noise. My ears began to hurt, so I held my nose and blew my ears clear. The noise was caused by shells passing me from the ground up to the next wave of bombers. This worried me, and I decided to hurry my descent by slipping air out of one side of my parachute. However, pulling on the risers almost collapsed it. Straightening out the cords, I got air back into my parachute and took my time going down.

After a few moments, I looked down to see that I was drifting toward a landing in a river. I was glad I was wearing my Mae West. Even if I got wet, I could float until getting to shore. But it sure looked cold! Fortunately, the wind changed and blew me south, away from the river. Some cleared land lay between a forest and some cliffs that fell steeply for about a thousand feet into the river. I looked for a good spot to land. As I got closer, I could see that the cleared land was about one-hundred feet wide. Then it dropped about twenty feet to another terrace of about twenty feet before the edge of the thousand-foot drop into the river.

Landing on the upper terrace, I was unable to dump my parachute before it dragged me over the first twenty-foot drop. But snow cushioned my fall, and my parachute collapsed before I did.

At once, armed men ran toward me. My apprehension turned to relief when the first to arrive helped me out of my parachute harness, rolled up the chute, and buried it in a snow bank. The next man to reach me spoke perfect English. He said they were friends and would help me, but we must move fast because the Germans were coming. They helped me up, and we had started towards the forest when a young lad ran up and spoke to the English-speaking man. They told me they wouldn't be able to get me away because there were too many Germans around us. The group was going to pretend they had captured me for the Germans in order to continue to help other fliers shot down. They asked that I give them my gun, knife, and money from my escape kit. Since I wasn't going to get away, I gave them the articles requested, knowing the Germans would take them anyway. I never saw the gun, knife, or money again. But neither did the German troops.

When the Germans arrived, it didn't take them long to find the parachute, which they made me carry to a road where a Jeep-like car met us to take me, along with a guard, to a nearby village. I was put into a local jail. Soon the copilot Lt. Burt Talcott showed up. Later our radioman Sgt. John Exarhakos arrived, horribly burned about the face. We called him Sergeant X because none of the crew could pronounce his Greek name. The last to appear was Sgt. Milton Plourde, the substitute flight engineer, who had quite a tale to tell. He had landed in the village pigpen and was covered in pig feces from being rolled around in the pen before being able to get his parachute off. He smelled too bad for the Germans to stand. They hosed him off, and then ordered him to remove all his clothing. They hosed him off again before he was given a hot shower and left in the shower room until the village women had washed and ironed his clothing.

He came into our cell looking as if he was ready for Saturday morning inspection.

Sergeant X and the engineer told us they had tried to get Sgt. Albert Wilson, the ball-turret gunner out, but the fire was too hot. Sgt. William Lemanski, the tail gunner, who in practice was always ready to bail out, had fought them when they tried to throw him out. They had to bail out without him. Lt. Edwin Feld, the pilot, being very short, needed help getting out the top hatch. Talcott helped him out, but Feld hit the horizontal stabilizer on the tail and never opened his chute. Talcott also hit the stabilizer, but it broke off. His only problem was that his parachute harness was too small for him, although it was the largest available. Therefore, he was in constant pain until he landed and was able to take off his chute. Apparently, Sgt. Reinaldo Garza, the upper turret gunner, along with Lemanski, Wilson, Turitz, and Rich went down with the plane. Why Turitz and Rich didn't follow me through the nose-wheel opening is still a mystery.

As I thought of those who didn't make it to the ground safely and reflected on my premonition, I felt lucky to be alive. But I really don't think it was just luck. The strong awareness of death before the mission, the narrow escape from death when the plane was hit, and my subsequent survival convinced me that I do indeed have a guardian angel.

The next day, an SS Officer, about seven feet tall, rousted us out of the jail and to an automobile. I was in the lead when he shoved me with his gun and told me to get into the back seat. I knew what he wanted, but I didn't want to get in. On the back seat was a machine gun, and I thought he wanted an excuse to shoot me, because I would then be armed. I backed up. He hit me with his gun and shouted, *"Rous!"* I threw my parachute over the machine gun. About this time, the driver sat up, shouted something, dove over the back of the seat, and burrowed under the parachute. He recovered his gun, gave a big sigh, and motioned me into the rear seat. I guessed it wasn't a trick after all.

The giant SS man chewed on the driver all the way to Klagenfurt. Then he told us, "For you, der var is ofver."

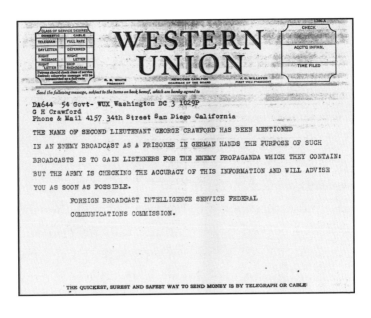

WESTERN UNION

DA644 54 Govt- WUX Washington DC 3 1029P
G H Crawford
Phone & Mail 4157 34th Street San Diego California

THE NAME OF SECOND LIEUTENANT GEORGE CRAWFORD HAS BEEN MENTIONED
IN AN ENEMY BROADCAST AS A PRISONER IN GERMAN HANDS THE PURPOSE OF SUCH
BROADCASTS IS TO GAIN LISTENERS FOR THE ENEMY PROPAGANDA WHICH THEY CONTAIN:
BUT THE ARMY IS CHECKING THE ACCURACY OF THIS INFORMATION AND WILL ADVISE
YOU AS SOON AS POSSIBLE.

      FOREIGN BROADCAST INTELLIGENCE SERVICE FEDERAL
      COMMUNICATIONS COMMISSION.

THE QUICKEST, SUREST AND SAFEST WAY TO SEND MONEY IS BY TELEGRAPH OR CABLE

INTERROGATION

When we arrived at Klagenfurt, we saw the devastation caused by our bombing. The railroad yards were a mess, but already crews of men and women were repairing the roadbeds and tracks. Some bombs had landed outside the target area. The big Goon guard told us that a kindergarten had been hit. I let him know that I had hit the marshaling yards. I hit what I aimed at!

We spent the night in a jail and left the next morning on a train just north of the city. Our boxcar was a 40-and-8, forty men or eight horses. It smelled like the horses had made the last trip before us. We four prisoners were put in one end of the boxcar, while the two guards were at the other end near a small stove. This was winter, and our captors had taken our flying clothes. It was bitterly cold, and snow was everywhere. The boxcar was drafty, but we were still alive.

The train made many stops on sidetracks to let the military trains rumble by. It took four days and nights to get to Frankfurt am Main, and we arrived during a bombing raid. Our guards locked us in the boxcar and said they were going to a bomb shelter. They would see us later, if we were still alive.

It is not pleasant knowing you are in the middle of a target during bombing raids. Near misses violently rocked our boxcar and threw it off the tracks into a ditch, but luckily we received no direct hits.

Even though we were hungry and thirsty, we finally got some sleep after the daylight raids by the Americans and the night raids by the British. The next morning the guards returned and pried open the boxcar door. We immediately demanded food and water but were told that we would have to take a little walk to a place where food and water were located.

It was quite a walk from the wrecks and ruins of the railroad yards, across the town of

Frankfurt, and up to a castle on top of the highest hill. This was Dulag Luft, the interrogation center for all downed aircrews.

During the whole trip, Sergeant X, despite his horrible wounds and oozing flesh, never complained of his pain. His only comments were to apologize for the odor from his burned flesh. His conduct was exemplary, his fortitude heroic.

During our march through Frankfurt, hate emanated from the civilians. We marched with heads erect, soldierly. I was proud of our military bearing.

Then our substitute engineer broke ranks to pick up a rotten potato from the gutter. He could have been shot during his short run, but he got back in the ranks before the guards could react. He wiped the loose dirt off the potato and proceeded to eat it. The fool didn't even know that there is no nourishment in such a potato. I thought his action was disgraceful.

When we entered the castle, each of us was taken to a different part of the dungeons.

Later, I was taken up some stairs to a very small cell about thirty feet above the ground level and was brought a slice of brown bread and a cup of ersatz coffee, my first food in five days. My cell was about four feet by six feet with a narrow bunk built along one side. I promptly sacked out. Shortly, I awoke to the smell of something burning. It was my jacket, charred by the heat from the wall behind the bunk. I rattled the door to get the attention of the jailer. When he finally came, I said, "It's too hot in this cell. Would you please turn down the heat?"

He explained, "Nothing in Frankfurt works right because of the bombing. I can't adjust the heat because the controls are broken. Furthermore, since it is your friends who broke the controls, you can just get used to the heat!"

The next morning brought another slice of bread and a cup of ersatz coffee before I was taken into an office for interrogation. A cordial German lieutenant offered me a cigarette from a new pack of Camels. I declined.

Then he inquired, " Where are you from in the USA, and where did you get your training?"

In accordance with the Geneva Convention, I replied, "My name is George G. Crawford, Second Lieutenant, serial number AO-753063."

He remarked, "The war is almost over, so you may as well relax and give me correct answers to my questions."

Again, name, rank, and serial number.

"Lieutenant, you are from San Diego. You went to school there, and I probably know as much about you as you do."

George G. Crawford

Again, name, rank, and serial number.

"You are being stupid! If you would cooperate, life would be a lot nicer for you."

As I started to repeat my name, rank, and serial number, he looked angry and got up. Going to a filing cabinet, he pulled out a file, shoved it toward me, and demanded, "Read this!"

I was shocked! He was right! He did know

all about me. There was my date and place of birth—August 9, 1920, St. Joseph's Hospital, San Diego. He had all my schools—grammar, junior high, high school, and San Diego State College. My whole life up to two days before being shot down was in this file!

He then told me that before the war, he had been a scriptwriter in Hollywood and had spent lots of time in San Diego and Tijuana. He told me details about San Diego that only a native would know, and then asked, "Now, are you ready to cooperate?"

Again, name, rank, and serial number. My mind was in turmoil. Our security must really be bad. All that information could have come only from Headquarters, U.S. Army Air Corps.

The German lieutenant lost interest in me, and a guard took me back to my cell. At least, the heat was off for now. After the war, I learned that baking a POW prior to interrogation was S.O.P. to weaken the POW. I'm glad I didn't know that before the interrogation. It might have weakened me.

STALAG LUFT III

The morning after the interrogation, I was ordered down to the castle's courtyard, where I joined my copilot and about forty other American flying officers. We were marched down to the railroad and into a 40-and-8 boxcar. It shouldn't have been crowded except that all of the POWs had to stay behind a line that divided the boxcar in half. One-half was for the POWs, and one-half for the two guards. The guards' half had a small coal-fired heater. After my trip from Klagenfurt with no food and little water, my pants were getting loose. All of us were losing weight. Our half of the boxcar was crowded and cramped. Consequently, the POWs had to take turns stretching out or sitting with their chins on their knees.

We arrived at Sagan, the town from which the invasion of Poland took place. More important to us, it was the town nearest to Stalag Luft

III, which was to be our home until January 1945. Our group was marched to the Vorlager of Stalag III where our fingerprints and photos were taken. Some photos! There had been no washing or shaving and not much food or beverage since being shot down. The photos were published to show the Germans what *Luftgangsters* looked like. We were issued a German dogtag in place of our American dogtags. The POW dogtag was about 2" x 3" of a pot-metal material. Perforations divided the dogtag lengthwise, and my Kriegie number 3774 was stamped on both sides of the perforations. A guard explained that should I die or be killed, the dogtag would be broken. One side would be sent to Dulag Luft to be recorded, and the other side would be placed in my mouth so that my body could be identified after the war was over.

The Goon then issued my eating utensils consisting of a bowl, cup, knife, fork, and spoon. Next, he gave me a very thin blanket, seven bed boards, and a palliasse, which is a burlap bag filled with shredded wood and used as a mattress. This completed my Kriegie inventory. I was told to take good care of each and every item, as none would be replaced.

The German Luft III Headquarters looked similar to the headquarters of one of our state or national parks, with neat buildings and rustic fences made of split rails. The POW compounds were not as attractive. The fences consisted of two parallel barbed-wire fences six feet apart and ten feet high. The horizontal strands were about six inches apart and securely fastened to the vertical strands, which were about two feet apart. The space between the fences was filled with coils of barbed wire. Twenty-four hours a day, guards with machine guns and huge searchlights manned tall guard towers placed about one-hundred yards apart. A boisterous crowd of American and British airmen yelling questions greeted our group after we were marched from the Vorlager to the Center Compound.

"Where were you shot down? Where are you from? What outfit were you in?"

None of the raucous questions could be answered over the roar of the crowd.

Before I left for overseas, my wife and I had talked with many friends. One of these was Barbara, whose husband Griff had met with unusually bad luck. Griff had piloted a B-25 on General Doolittle's raid over Japan. After bombing Japan, Griff had flown over the China Sea where he and his crew bailed out when the plane's fuel was exhausted.

It took Griff six months to get back to the USA. His next tour was in the European Theater of Operations, where he was soon shot down and reported to be a POW. I had told Barbara that I would convey her messages to Griff if I had the misfortune to be made a POW and met up with him. Griff was the first person I saw inside the Center Compound of Stalag III. I conveyed Barbara's messages of love and affection.

The Center Compound was the oldest compound and had been occupied by British N.C.O.s who had managed to practically destroy the barracks by removing most of the inner walls to use for firewood. When American POWs became more numerous, due to the increasing number of B-17s and B-24s being shot down after August 1943, the Germans started constructing additional compounds. When the North, East, and South Compounds were constructed, the British moved out of the Center Compound.

The newer compounds, I was told, had rooms built within the larger barracks, thereby providing better protection from the bitter cold of German winters. The Center Compound was never repaired, leaving cracks through which the wind gusted until closed by snow and icicles. Germany had one month of spring, one month of summer, one month of fall, and nine months of winter.

Each new Kriegie was quarantined until he was identified by one of the previously cleared Kriegies. This could be a difficult time for a new crew from the USA who had followed the false German radio beam used to lead them to land in occupied France rather than in England. They had to undergo a more intense interrogation than the one at Dulag Luft. This was necessary to weed out the false Kriegies planted by the Germans. I had no difficulty, as San Diego had as many Kriegies in Stalag Luft III as most of the states had. San Diego was really a military town!

I was assigned to a "combine" consisting of six to eight Kriegies who arranged the bunks and lockers around a designated area to simulate a room separate from other combines in the large barn-like barracks. Each barrack in Center Compound had only two small rooms. One was designated the kitchen; the other was for the senior officer in the barrack.

I was given a middle bunk and immediately made it useful by placing my seven boards in place and laying the palliasse on the boards with the one thin blanket on top. The bunks were layered so close together that one had to be approximately horizontal to sinuously slither into the bunk. There was no room to sit up in bed. Not too comfortable, but better than nothing. I then put the bowl, cup, knife, fork, and spoon in the locker assigned to me. It looked mighty empty. I was told that my rations would arrive soon, but, except for the cigarettes and a chocolate "D" bar, all the rest would go into the combine's locker from where it would be prepared by the "cook of the week."

When the Red Cross food parcel arrived, it consisted of one can of Spam, one can of sardines or salmon, one can of corned beef, one can of margarine, one can of orange-juice powder, one can of Nescafe, one small box of "C" ration crackers, one box of prunes, one small box of sugar cubes, one "D" bar, and one pack of six cigarettes.

Our combine of eight Kriegies took turns with the chores and duties. Some were better or more imaginative cooks. The limited variety and supply of food challenged even the most ingenious cooks. Each week, every Kriegie was issued one-half of a Red Cross parcel. A loaf of bread, weighing seven pounds, was made with one-fourth mixed-grain flour, one-half potato flour, and one-fourth wood pulp. Also, we received one pound of potatoes, usually rotten, as well as several pounds of kohlrabi, which were not edible no matter how they were prepared. In the summer, we received one-half head of cabbage and the equivalent amount of sauerkraut in the winter. If a cow or horse died close to camp, we received one piece of meat about two inches square per month. If no fresh meat was available, blood sausage was substituted. Unfortunately, the blood leaked all over.

Since all food was used in common in the combine, except the "D" bar and the small package of six cigarettes, which each Kriegie kept separately, these items were the camp currency. The above food, together with one cup of German soup, usually barley or split pea fortified with weevils, furnished about one thousand calories per day until October 1944, when rations were cut. In October 1944, I weighed 38.5 kgs., or 85 pounds. When liberated, I weighed 29.5 kgs., or 65 pounds, according to camp scales.

Another item rationed was toilet paper. Each Kriegie was issued one four-inch square of paper per day. The German paper had splinters, which had to be removed before use. This was a hardship at first, but because of the shortage of food and the change of our digestive tracts, the feces were soon pellets similar to deer droppings.

To avoid arguments over the division of food in the combine, the cook had the task of dividing the cooked food into equal portions. To ensure the equality of food division, the order of choosing plates was rotated each day except for the cook, who always took last.

Each Kriegie developed some personal skill, which was used to trade for a chore he disliked. I became a barber, in demand because of my efforts to please my customers. This was not easy with only scissors and hand clippers. I was amazed by some styles requested, but it didn't matter, because no one was going anywhere soon.

Besides barbering, cooking, cleaning, and a short time gardening, which was ended by the Goons, who thought I was digging an escape tunnel, I spent most of my time reading books from the extensive library the YMCA managed to get into our compound. My greatest pleasure was derived from smoking a pipeload of English tobacco, purchased with my American cigarettes, while reading an interesting book. The tobacco deadened the hunger; the book provided me with a form of escape from Stalag Luft III.

The YMCA managed to supply the many talented musicians in our compound with a complete selection of band instruments. We had Kriegies who played with the Big Bands–Benny Goodman, Tommy and Jimmy Dorsey, and Stan Kenton. The band concerts were Standing Room Only, except for the American and German generals who never missed a concert and always had a seat. Listening to the orchestra was a great experience, taking most of us back to college days where we danced with beautiful coeds to fabulous music.

Mail call was the most eagerly awaited moment of camp life. It offered a message of love and hope from home. Occasionally, especially in the British compounds, a "Dear John" letter brought great despair as a wife or sweetheart decided not to wait for a Kriegie to return home. Despite knowing that my wife and other members of my family were writing as often as they could, I received only two letters from my wife, both heavily censored by two armies with lines or sections cut out. No letters ever arrived from the rest of my family.

We Kriegies were allowed to write letters on special forms that were rationed. I spent hours trying to devise a code my wife could figure out without the censors getting wise. I thought I had succeeded, but since most of my letters to my wife arrived after I got home, the effort turned out to be only an exercise to occupy my time. Even I couldn't remember or decode the letters, so most were never read.

But always uppermost on our minds was food or the lack thereof. We discussed imaginary menus. We created lists of our favorite foods and methods of preparation. We dreamed about future feasts, but none nourished our bodies.

When Surrender Was Not An Option

THE OPERATIONAL FUNCTION

Kriegies' thoughts, conversations, and activities could be divided into three main categories—home, food, or escape. Thoughts and activities regarding escape could be divided into two categories—death, or causing the Third Reich as much trouble as possible. Kriegies within the first category were quite obvious. They would come into camp, look around for friends, and evaluate the plus or minus of POW life. Next they would clean their clothing and their bodies, visit the chaplain, and then lie down on their bunks and die. Usually, they were dead within forty-eight hours. Their escape was quick and final.

Those in the other category, which included most Kriegies, were of the opinion that escaping was the "operational function" of the Kriegie. "Operational" meant that the fight that they had trained for was not over. They were back in the war fighting the enemy. They had a chance to disrupt the war effort of the Third Reich, not only as individuals but also as a team. Even a Kriegie who never considered escaping as an individual could contribute by helping one of his fellow Kriegies to escape. All efforts toward escaping caused the Germans to increase the number of guards, thereby reducing the number of soldiers on the front lines. Each escape caused the Germans to mobilize hundreds of soldiers and thousands of police and civilian volunteers.

Escape activity, better known in Stalag Luft III as "X" activity, was a highly organized, coordinated, and sophisticated art. Our "X" activity, which had many facets, took a semi-neutral Kriegie and put him back to work. There was work for each Kriegie whatever his talent, and with 10,000 Kriegies in Stalag III, all talents were available. Many of the airmen in the compound had completed at least two years of college. And being men hardened by the Great Depression, most of them possessed exceptional mental fortitude and resourcefulness.

Security was most important for all "X" activities. Consequently, we developed a "duty pilot system" to keep "X" activities secure. We located the duty pilot where he could observe all Germans entering or leaving the camp. He possessed sketches of all known personnel, especially the "Ferrets" who were anti-escape specialists who prowled under, over, and through the barracks. The Goons were the members of the camp staff. The "duty pilot" also had Kriegie runners who kept the Ferrets and Goons under constant observation while they were in camp and thus were able to warn all Kriegies who were engaged in "X" activities.

The Germans knew we kept a logbook on them. They didn't approve but couldn't do anything about it. It became sort of a joke. Some of the Goons would even check in with the "duty pilot" when entering or leaving camp. When the German Kommandant inquired as to the meaning of "Goon," we told him it meant "German Officers or Non-Coms." Since he was not familiar with American comics, the explanation satisfied him.

Most escapes necessitated tunnels, which required much talent and many man-hours of labor. Our Kriegie engineers discovered primitive seismographs surrounding the perimeter of our camp and microphones buried about seven feet deep about every twenty feet. We made this discovery only after the Germans kept finding and destroying several tunnels. The solution to this problem was to dig the shafts twenty- to thirty-feet deep before heading the horizontal tunnels toward the fences. We also dug dummy tunnels so the Germans could discover and destroy them. This kept them happy and not too alert.

Since the barracks were mounted on pilings high enough to allow the Ferrets to prowl beneath them, one problem was the location of a secure shaft head. One solution was to begin the shaft in an open space, reinforce the shaft with a trap door about two feet below the surface and hide it with dirt piled on top. Another solution was to use one of the tile-covered concrete foundations that supported large, heavy charcoal stoves.

We removed the stove, dug a shaft through the concrete, and constructed a trap door. Then we covered the trap door with concrete and tile and placed the stove over it. Whenever the Germans were around, we kept a fire burning in the stove. If an emergency occurred with an unexpected inspection when a Kriegie was digging in the tunnel, the stove could be replaced, and the stove-pipe extension constructed of klim cans could disappear. It only took about one minute to make the change, even with a hot, heavy stove.

One of the cleverest locations for a successful tunnel was in East Compound. The Kriegies built a Trojan Horse, a large, wood vaulting horse open on the bottom. The Kriegies would carry the Trojan horse out to the same spot on the exercise field every day and continuously vault until the Kriegie digger had filled the twelve bags inside the horse. The digger dug straight down, reinforcing the shaft and placing a trap door over the shaft head then covering all with sand. The athletes would then carry the Trojan horse, the digger, and twelve bags of soil back to the barracks where the sand would be dispersed. This was a slow but successful operation. By this means, three Kriegies escaped to England.

The most difficult part of tunneling in a POW camp was the disposal of the dirt. At first, it was placed in attics until one of the barracks collapsed. It was then placed in the big toilet called an abort until it overflowed. The final and most successful solution was to use "Penguins." A Penguin was a Kriegie carrying two bags of soil suspended inside his pants. Each bag was fastened on the bottom by a pin attached to a string, which the Penguin could pull and allow the dirt to be disguised by blending with the surface of the camp. I discovered that the surface of Center Camp had been raised three feet the summer I planted a garden. I had to dig down three feet to get to the topsoil.

The tunnels were primitive at first, but after several cave-ins they were reinforced with bed boards. Air was furnished to the tunnel head with bellows made from kit bags through a pipe made of klim cans buried in the tunnel floor. At first, the only light was a candle burning refined margarine with wicks made from pajama cords, but after we stole four hundred feet of cable left by some German workers, we had electric lights by tying into the German lines.

Tunneling was only the basic part of "X" activities. Light-fingered Kriegies, also known as pickpockets, could remove wallets and papers from Ferrets and Goons, photograph the contents and return the wallets and papers before the Ferrets and Goons had completed the inspection of the barracks.

Then skillful forgers would prepare papers, passes, money and identification documents that could pass scrutiny. One complicated paper with an extraordinary background took one forger, working five hours a day, a month to complete. Of course, we did have time to complete tasks.

Talented tailors comprised another group of Kriegies. They were able to create German uniforms, workers' coveralls and civilian clothing, using some of the most ingenious methods imaginable. Materials came from many resources. Dyes were obtained from medicines, tea, coffee, and bookbindings. Pouring molten foil from cigarette packages or lead created some buckles, buttons, and badges. Others were formed from melting the beads of solder on tin cans and pouring it into molds and casts made from soap or plaster of Paris obtained from the sick bay. Paper, cardboard, and wood were colored with shoe polish to resemble belts, holsters, and even guns. Some blankets were received that had concealed patterns of civilian suits. One RAF man received a uniform from home that was a cleverly disguised *Luftwaffe* uniform.

One "X" committee provided maps, including for us everyday Kriegies a huge war map that was hung on a wall. Battle lines changed daily and were marked with colored yarn. It was so accurate that the Goons compared it to the propaganda they received. They knew we had to have radios to have such accurate battle news, but they never discovered where we hid them. They didn't try too hard to find them after D-Day.

Another necessity for escape was a compass. These were made from a 78-RPM phonograph record. A disk was cut out, heated and molded into a case. The bottom of a case held a piece of cardboard with a phonograph needle embedded in the middle. A strip of magnetized razor blade indicated north, another example of American ingenuity.

Although several small individual escapes were unsuccessful, all "X" activity operated smoothly. The Germans sentenced the recaptured Kriegies to thirty days in the "kooler," solitary confinement with only bread and water.

Then came the Great Escape! On the evening of March 24 and the morning of March 25, 1944, seventy-six Kriegies made it out of the tunnel before it was discovered. Twenty-two were captured almost immediately and were subsequently dispersed among other prison camps. Fifty-four got away from the environs of Sagan. Three escaped to

England by stealing boats, drifting down rivers to the sea and hiding on Swedish ships with the cooperation of the crews. The remaining fifty-one were eventually captured. The Gestapo shot fifty. One Kriegie was returned to the South Camp. Since he was not shot, we assumed that he was a plant, and no one ever spoke to him again. Because this harsh and illegal execution of fifty Kriegies was a clear violation of the Geneva Convention, twenty-one members of the Gestapo involved in the killings were tried and executed after the war.

General Vanaman, our Senior American Officer, cautioned us concerning "X" activities. In October 1944, the Allied Headquarters in London announced that escape was no longer a duty. Despite the announcement, most of us continued to harass the enemy until liberated.

Time dragged on. Rations got short. We knew the Germans were losing the war. The *Luftwaffe* was being destroyed. The British and Americans were approaching from the west. The Russians were racing from the east. The question in all of the Kriegies' minds was, "What are the Germans planning for us?"

Christmas 1944 was depressing, even though we "bashed" to celebrate. It had been snowing forever. The temperature in the barracks was below zero degrees. We were tired of short rations, chilblains, no heat, and everlasting dampness. Rumors abounded. We developed emergency plans in case Hitler ordered our extermination. Increasing the perimeter of our compound, we tried to plan for any eventuality by saving food, repairing shoes, converting clothing into knapsacks, making maps, and keeping up-to-date battle maps. The Goons left the maps alone for they wanted to see the true situation. But that was the only thing they left alone. They took any food beyond three-days' supply. Knapsacks were confiscated. Chaos reigned. What would happen? Were we to be left behind when the Goons left? Were we to be liquidated? Marched out? Taken by truck or train?

MOVING OUT

On January 27, 1945, at about 9:00 P.M., with a blizzard blowing and the temperature about minus twenty degrees, the Goons told us to get ready to move out. We could hear the thunder and see the flashes from the Russian artillery. More rumors abounded. One rumor was that his German friends had offered General Vanaman, who had been in the U.S. Embassy in Berlin from 1937 to 1941, a chauffeur-driven staff car. That rumor was true. However, General Vanaman refused the offer, stating that he was going to march at the head of his troops, and when he got tired, his troops would be tired, and they would all stop and rest awhile. General Vanaman was about twice as old as the rest of us, a real commanding officer!

At the same time that we were told to get ready to leave Stalag III, it was suggested that we arrange a "buddy" system. Two Kriegies could help each other on the forthcoming march. It sounded like a good idea. I weighed eighty-five pounds at this time. Therefore, I reasoned that a newer Kriegie who hadn't lost much weight would make the ideal "buddy." I located one of the newest arrivals, a "Little All-American" football player from West Virginia, who looked healthy and husky enough to be of help to me on the march.

General Vanaman and Colonel Spivey, the senior American officers, had been worried about the future food situation for some time and had held back on the distribution of the American Red Cross food parcels in order to have a supply should shipments cease. A large supply had been created.

When the orders came to march, we each had one thin blanket, a small supply of food and two pairs of socks. We wore the rest of our clothing. As we were leaving camp, we were issued two complete boxes of Red Cross food parcels as rations for the march. Unfortunately, most of the

Kriegies were too weak to carry the extra weight. As a result, all along the line of march, they discarded various items. The hard march in the blizzard and struggle through the deep snow while trying to carry the extra weight of the food parcels caused some Kriegies to fall out. Attempting to lighten the load, most Kriegies ate as much of the food as they could as a way to carry it and still benefit from it. Still, many of the food items were discarded.

Trudging up a hill, we stopped to get our breath. My feet were in bad shape. The Goons for some unknown reason had taken my shoes from me but had left my flight boots, which were lined with sheepskin. Without shoes inside, the flight boots were too large and provided no support for walking. When we stopped, I put on all my socks to take up the space inside the boot. Although the boots were still loose, they were not falling off at every step.

The cold was very bitter, and as we rested, we got colder. Looking back at Stalag III, we saw flames shooting skyward. Some of the Kriegies had left incendiary devices hidden in the barracks to prevent the Goons from obtaining any advantage from marching us out. Apparently no one was trying to put out the fires. We could have used the heat where we were. But we faced two choices— march or die. To keep alive, we started marching again.

Boxes of dried prunes were among the numerous items discarded. The guards, whose rations were usually sausage, cheese, and black bread, were delighted to see the bounty of dried fruit and reaped an unexpected harvest. They filled their knapsacks with as many boxes as could be stuffed into them. When their knapsacks were full, they filled their stomachs with dried prunes.

The next day, the guards learned the result of eating several pounds of prunes. All Kriegies could have escaped while the guards were helpless while squatting alongside the road with their pants around their ankles, but our senior American officers ordered us not to escape.

My bright idea of getting a new Kriegie to buddy with soon proved to be a "bummer." Beginning about two kilometers out of Sagan he complained about pains and wanted me to carry his pack at about four kilometers. I expected more from a "Little All American" who weighed over two times as much as I did and was less than one-half the age of General Vanaman at the head of our troops. I tried to carry his pack but knew that with the cold and my lack of strength, I couldn't last long with double packs.

Some Polish laborers were about fifty feet from our line of march, and they had some sleds. I thought that pulling a double load on a sled would be easier, and since I had a supply of cigarettes to barter with, I left the line of march to bargain for the sled. Just as I opened negotiations, a German lieutenant arrived and ordered me back to the line of march. The Goon lieutenant wouldn't listen to my explanation. I started back to the column, but as soon as his back was turned, I returned to the bargaining, which I halted when I felt the muzzle of his Walther pistol behind my ear. I hurried back to the line of march and told my buddy that I couldn't carry his load any farther. Rather than carry his own load, he collapsed by the side of the road.

We marched about eighteen kilometers that day, but the trek seemed longer because of the cold and our physical condition. We were supposed to march for one hour then take a five-minute rest. I guess those Kriegies in the front of the column marched one hour and then got a five-minute rest, but those of us from the middle to the back of the column never got a rest. With about 10,000 Kriegies strung out, the line of march expanded like an accordion and then closed up during the rest period of those in front. The result was that those Kriegies not in the front only rested when they collapsed. I kept thinking of General Vanaman, that old man in the front. If he could do it, so could I!

We finally reached Halbau that evening, still cold, exhausted, and wondering what tomorrow

Out

ing?

ings

ped

our

and

urch

and

the

icult

ntil

tions

e to

ived

oor

not

g as

When Surrender

MARCHING

The next day brought a little change in the weather. It had warmed up to about thirty degrees below zero, and there was no wind nor extreme chill factor. Still, it was cold enough to freeze the hinges of the gates of Hell, and most of us were glad to get out of the church and to stretch the kinks out of our muscles. We got on with our march through the minus-thirty-degree weather and hoped to have a better place to rest that night.

Many of the Kriegies were suffering from frozen toes, but no one dropped out of the line of march because of that. A rumor that the Goons were stacking all Kriegie stiffs along the side of the road to wait for the frozen ground to thaw before burying them kept some of the Kriegies marching. My motivation was to not let the Goons get the best of me, and besides, the Old Man was still leading us.

It was cold and getting colder. The rate of travel seemed to be slowing down. The shoes of some Kriegies were cracking and separating from their soles. At each rest stop, the Kriegies rubbed margarine into the leather to try to keep the moisture on the outside of the shoes. Even though my flight boots seemed to be getting heavier and heavier, and it was difficult walking in them, I realized that I was a lucky one because the Goons had taken my shoes instead of my flight boots. Walking in them was sloppy, but my feet were not freezing. Yet, I was cold; everyone was cold. My breath froze on the towel that I used as a muffler around my neck and chin, but it provided extra protection.

Confusion among the Goons halted our march. There was much running back and forth by the Supermen. Maybe the war was over, maybe not. At least, we had a chance to rest a bit and break out what remained of our rations. Some Kriegies were bemoaning the food they had discarded because they had been too weak to carry it. Soon the word passed down the line of march.

The stupid Goons had taken a wrong turn in the road, and we would have to march cross-country to get to the right road. The Kriegies in the front had some trouble with the deep snow, but since I was so far back in the line, the snow was well packed by the time we got to turn off. If only my flight boots had fit better!

While going cross-country, we passed some very small villages, a church, and a few farmhouses. We saw only very old people or very young children. Some of the villagers stood by the side of the road with pots of hot water to offer to the Kriegies. We knew they were taking chances by being kind to Kriegies. Sure enough! Some S S troops and local policemen soon chased them back into their homes.

This was just another example of the mindset of the damn Nazi! We had learned that the professional German soldier was an honorable man who would comply with the Geneva Convention as well as he was able to. We also learned that religion was still alive in Germany—at least, in the villages.

But the Gestapo, the S S, and the Hitler Youth were a bunch of bloody bastards.

We continued to march through the falling snow, but we seemed to be getting nowhere. Telling time was difficult, for we had no sun during the miserable day that grew darker and colder. Some complained and cursed, but I saved my breath and strength by keeping quiet. My thoughts, however, were not pleasant. But I kept hoping we would reach our destination for the night. I was getting tired, very tired. I wondered how much farther General Vanaman could keep on going.

Finally, we were just about *kaput* when we came to a larger village called Barrau. Some of the residents offered to let the Kriegies into their homes for shelter. Some were actually in the homes when the S S and the police searched each home and chased the Kriegies out into the sub-zero weather. About four kilometers farther, we reached some large barns that were about fifty feet by one-hundred and fifty feet. The Goons ordered about six-hundred Kriegies into each barn.

To my surprise, I learned that from Halbau to Barrau was only fourteen kilometers, but of course we went much farther, due to the Goons' taking the wrong turn. I climbed into a loft, knowing that heat rises, and gathered some hay for a bed in a corner of the loft. I lay down. The chance to rest, relax, and get warm was heavenly. I nibbled on a "C" ration cracker, ate a piece of a "D" bar and went to sleep after securing my rations within my coat and placing it under my head. One more day, and the Goons hadn't beaten me or General Vanaman yet.

BREAK TIME

Snowflakes slowly drifted down from a gray overcast as the new day dawned. I awoke to the sound of too many men in too small a space getting ready for another day of slogging through the snow. Most of the men went into the barnyard to relieve themselves. Others, who still had some food, nibbled on a piece of a "D" bar or a "C" ration cracker. Since no water was available, we looked for clean snow to quench our thirst. Although I hated to leave my small semi-warm spot in the corner of the loft, I started to store my possessions in a pack and get ready for another day of marching through the snow.

Suddenly, a rumor spread through our barn that we were not going to leave today. We were going to have a day of rest! I couldn't believe it. I had heard too many false rumors, so I wasn't going to leave my corner in the loft until it was confirmed or proven false.

Then the good news came! No marching today! General Vanaman defied the Goons and refused to march. He kept his promise that he made when he refused to ride in a car while we marched! He said that when he was tired, his troops would be tired, and all of us would rest! We were all grateful that we had a senior American officer with the guts to defy the Goons and the integrity to protect his men. What a man!

After resting a while longer, I decided that this was a chance to use some of my carefully hoarded rations that needed to be cooked. About a month before the march, I had an attack of yellow jaundice and was placed in the infirmary. My only treatment was a change of diet. A steady diet of oatmeal changed my skin color from yellow back to normal, indicating a cure. When I left the infirmary, the flight surgeon gave me several small cans of compressed oatmeal to use if I noticed any more symptoms of jaundice. I had opened the cans and stored the oatmeal in a clean sock to lighten the load for our march. Now there was time to cook some oatmeal. I took a klim can and packed fresh snow in it, gathered some straw and scraps of wood, and built a small fire on the dirt floor of the barn. When the snow melted and the water boiled, I sprinkled some oatmeal into the klim can and stirred in a sugar cube. After it cooled, I spooned every flake of oatmeal into my mouth. What a treat! Some Kriegies tried to trade me out of some oatmeal, but I was selfish. I wouldn't trade. My stomach approved the best meal I had had in several days. Perhaps it was mostly psychological, but I felt much stronger and ready for another day of marching.

We rested all day—luxuriously. At least, it seemed like luxury. It was far better than marching in the snow for hours on end with aching muscles, chilblained feet, and nothing to satisfy our hunger and thirst.

The Goons rousted us out while it was still dark the next morning. Although we had had a day of rest, we were still tired and stiff. The Goons said we had to make up for the lost time and distance. The guards who had consumed too many dried prunes had recovered and didn't appreciate the comments and questions concerning their problems. They set a quick pace, and some Kriegies were not up to it and dropped out. Fortunately, General Vanaman had convinced the Goons to get a horse-drawn farm wagon to follow us for the weaker Kriegies to hitch a ride. This was an improvement over freezing to death by the side of the road, but many of the passengers developed frozen fingers, feet, and noses. Marching was not easy, but it kept the blood flowing and prevented some freezing of body parts.

The Goons kept up the fast pace, and the length of the line of march kept getting longer as the weaker and slower Kriegies kept falling back. Soon the horse-drawn wagon was full, causing a time limit to be placed on how long a Kriegie could ride on the wagon. We trudged on as the cold increased. The Goons promised us a nice warm place to sleep that night if we kept up the pace. Of course, we didn't believe them because of their pattern of false promises. They gave us neither new rations nor hot water on the march. Mostly, we didn't receive any water at all. I was tired and hungry, but as long as General Vanaman led us, I knew I could keep going. The Goons didn't look too good themselves, as most were older soldiers who had suffered wounds or disabilities.

The cold was harsh. We marched. The day grew darker. We marched. I ached from hunger. We marched. My feet and legs throbbed. We marched. The wind slashed my face. We marched. Kriegies groaned and moaned. We marched. More Kriegies collapsed. We marched. The cold grew bitter. We marched. Darkness set in. Still we marched.

Finally, a town came into sight. Surely, it had to be the place where we could stop for the night. It was! The Geneva Convention provided that POWs could not be marched farther than twenty kilometers, or twelve and one-half miles per day. We arrived at this town of Muskau, having marched thirty-four kilometers from Barrau! But the Goons did keep their promise of a warm place to stay. They packed us into a pottery factory that was still operating and making pottery. One-half of the factory was not in operation, and it was into this half that we were packed where the temperature was about thirty-five degrees.

When I entered the cool side of the factory, I just kept on walking toward the heat on the other side until it got too hot. I found a place where I could stand the heat if I stripped down to my shorts and boots. I thought that was pretty close to heaven. I claimed a spot for my own and dried out the snow and sweat from my clothing. The heat was wonderful! It dawned on me that if I went a little farther into the factory, I should be able to boil water. I found a water spigot, filled my klim can, and found a vent hot enough to boil water. Then I added oatmeal, klim, and sugar. What a feast!

Everything looked a lot better!

A CLOSE CALL

G ood news and feeling great! The good news was that we were going to have a full day to rest in the pottery factory. Feeling great resulted from a breakfast of oatmeal following a night's sleep in a warm place.

With time to spare in a warm place and a klim can of hot water, I cleaned up and even shaved for the first time since we started the march. At General Vanaman's urging, the Goons found food for us. Each of us was issued a quarter loaf of black bread, one-half pound of margarine, and about two tablespoons of barley soup—weevils and all. Because of my prior bout with jaundice, I was afraid to eat the margarine. My flight boots didn't need a coat of grease, and since everyone already had some, I couldn't trade it for something useful. Such a waste!

Most of the other Kriegies cleaned up themselves and their gear, repacked their few possessions that they had been able to retain, and then "sacked out."

Something's up! They got us up early for the road again, but the next day was another day of rest, and rest in a warm place had certainly helped us. Thank God for General Vanaman, his concern for his troops, and his contacts in Berlin. I know that without him, some of us wouldn't have made it even this far.

They gave us another German ration of one-half pound of margarine and one-half cup of barley soup. I drank the soup but refused the margarine. It was no good for trading, and I didn't want to carry it in my pack.

Then came the bad news. Rumor had it that the Goons were going to take our senior officers from us, by force if necessary, and move them to Berlin. The reason was unknown. Some guessed they would be taken to Switzerland to arrange the surrender of the Nazis. Others were of the opinion that they would be used as highly placed hostages to ensure the safety of German big shots.

Still others were certain they were removed so they would not be present when the rest of us were liquidated. The rumor that they would be taken from our group was true. They disappeared that day. Without General Vanaman, what would happen?

The following day we marched without General Vanaman, Colonel Spivey, and a few other senior officers. The weather had warmed, and the snow was melting. The roads were muddy, with pools of water here and there. Since the shoes of most of the Kriegies were falling apart, their feet were wet all the time.

The morale of both the Kriegies and the Goons began to disintegrate. Tempers were short; marching slowed. About dusk, we arrived at Graustein, where we were housed in barns for the night. Depression descended over us—no jokes, no comments, no razzing the Goons. All was quiet. We had lost our leaders and their protection. A vicious rumor started that our senior officers had bailed out on us to save their own lives. I didn't believe it, but was too tired to combat it.

Completing our eighth day on the road, we arrived at Spremberg where we were placed in 40-and-8 boxcars with about one hundred Kriegies in each boxcar. Although confined in cramped and totally unpleasant quarters, we soon found that there was nothing we could do about it.

Still, we were not the worst off. On a siding next to our train, stood a cattle car loaded with people much worse off than the Kriegies. Pale-gray skeletons with deep-set eyes begged us for food. I threw a piece of bread to a man's outstretched hand. As he caught it, a guard struck his arm with a blow of his rifle. The arm snapped, and the bread dropped to the cinders. The guard growled at the miserable prisoner as he slowly dragged his broken arm back inside the cattle car. We all glared with hatred at the Goon, but we didn't throw the prisoners anything else. It was not worth their pain and suffering.

Inside our 40-and-8, we could survive by taking turns either standing or sitting on the floor with our chins on our knees. We exchanged positions every half-hour. The train rolled down the tracks that evening with frequent stops on sidings to allow German troop trains to speed by. Hours later in the night, when my legs became cramped, I worked my way out of the boxcar and stood on the coupling between the cars.

From an adjacent car, an English POW with the same idea approached. We introduced ourselves. I asked him how long he had been imprisoned.

"Nearly four years," he replied.

Referring to my last name, he asked if I had been back to Scotland where my family had come from.

"I'm not a Scot," I informed him. "I'm Irish. My granddad came from Ireland to Pennsylvania and then around the Horn to California."

He told me he had been a Fellow at Oxford, and that genealogy was his specialty and life interest. He proceeded to lecture me on the Crawford Sept of the Lindsey Clan. I didn't dispute his discourse; in fact, I enjoyed it. We parted friends and returned to our respective boxcars.

In the early morning, a massive formation of our heavy bombers, escorted by P-51 fighters, passed overhead on their way to bomb the enemy. We knew that after bombing inner Germany and turning back to England, the fighters would drop down and strafe anything and everything moving. We were a target of opportunity.

P-51 Fighter Plane
Courtesy American Airpower Heritage Museum, Inc., Midland, TX

Fortunately, the German train engineer was also aware of the probability of being strafed. Below the level of the roadway where the track followed a ravine, he stopped the train. The guards set up a perimeter about a hundred-yard distance from the train, allowing the Kriegies to seek protection within the area. As I had earlier noticed a drainage ditch by the side of the road, I hurried up the slope to the roadway. I figured that the efficient Germans with all their slave labor had probably also placed another drainage ditch on the far side. I was right. I jumped into the ditch farthest from the train.

We didn't have long to wait. We could hear the P-51s coming with their guns firing, their shells hitting the train, and the hiss of steam escaping from the locomotive. I hugged the ground, but as the P-51s roared overhead, I looked up. For a moment, I froze as I saw the planes turn around to make another pass at the train. In my location, I had no protection. I decided to make a run for the ditch on the other side of the road. As I raised my head to start my sprint, I saw another flight of P-51s following the same path as the first wave. Oh, hell! No matter where I went, I was about to be shot by an American! What a way to go after all I had been through.

Fortunately, somehow, someone in the formation became aware that their target was a POW train. Both attacks were suddenly called off. The P-51 formations flew off after saluting us with dipped wings. I couldn't move. I just sat up and breathed deeply. That was too close!

Remarkably, there was only one casualty. An English POW decided to brew a cup of tea. As he was drawing hot water from the locomotive during the attack, a shell hit his shoulder and tore off his arm. Our flight surgeon attempted to stem the flow of blood, but it didn't look too good for our English friend.

The German engineer was busy chopping branches off a willow tree growing near the tracks. With his ax he shaped them and then drove them into the holes in the locomotive's steam boiler. Somehow, when we Kriegies were back in the boxcars, he got up enough steam to take us to the next station. There, a different locomotive was hitched to our train and we were again on our way. But where?

DOCTOR AZORIN

Early the next morning, our POW train stopped in a small station to take on water and fuel for the locomotive. We tried to clean up our boxcars, but not much was accomplished. It was a hopeless task with so many Kriegies crowded together. The day passed with many stops on sidings to yield to troop trains and flat cars carrying German tanks and 88s toward the front. Just before sunset, we stopped outside a small town where several horse-drawn wagons were waiting. What a surprise! The wagons contained a supply of cans of meat, each can weighing about two pounds. Each Kriegie was issued one can and warned that this had to last for five days, at which time we would be at our next camp.

The issue of cans raised morale, as most of us had been out of food for a couple of days. Two problems existed. One was how to open the can without a knife; the second was how to keep the opened can from spoiling in our filthy surroundings. One guard let us use his small can opener, one by one, while he watched to keep it secure. We were grateful for its use. It solved the first problem. I measured the can and marked off five portions on the outside of the can so that I could ration my food for five days. After opening my can, I saw chunks of meat, probably horse, surrounded by congealed fat.

Then I proceeded to eat my first day's ration of meat and fat. I knew that I should not eat the fat, but my starved body overruled my mental strength. I ate the meat and the fat. It tasted delicious! About two hours later, a consuming desire to eat again overcame me. I rationalized that savages ate huge amounts of food whenever it was available to make up for the periods of no food, even starvation. We were pretty close to being savages in our present surroundings. Maybe the savages were right to carry and store food within their bodies. At least, the food would not turn bad that way. They did not seem to suffer from such bash-ing. I didn't want my can of food to turn rancid, and besides, the meat and fat tasted so good. I could not resist eating just a little bit more of the meat and fat.

Suddenly my can of meat and fat was empty. I couldn't believe that the meat was all gone! I didn't remember eating so much, but it was all gone! Oh well, my stomach felt full, and I fell asleep when it was my turn to sit.

I woke up with a start. I was nauseated and felt the need to vomit. There was no place to vomit. We were so crowded that I would have to vomit on my fellow Kriegies. Then I noticed the small open window above my head. Here was the answer. I would chin myself on the bottom of the window and vomit outside the boxcar.

I chinned myself and vomited outside. Immediately, I felt my gut muscles pull loose, and the pain was so severe that I screamed and fell to the floor. It felt like everything in my guts had torn loose. Some of them had. I lay on the floor and stayed there until morning. The train stopped. The senior American officer believed I was dying; the German guard agreed. I was left behind with one guard when the train pulled out.

The powers-that-be ruled that I should seek medical care at one of the five German army hospitals in the near vicinity. There was no transportation. The guard and I slowly walked to the hospital. I discovered that the pain was less severe if I held in my bulging abdomen with two hands. Apparently, I had suffered a hernia or rupture of some kind. It was difficult to carry my bedroll with my few possessions packed while holding my abdomen, but the guard did not hurry me.

The hospital staff told the guard that they were over-crowded with wounded German soldiers, and that they had no room for a *Luftgangster*. The second, third, fourth, and fifth hospitals also turned the *Luftgangster* away. The guard was becoming disturbed; he didn't like being turned away. He set me down and told me not to leave as he went into a building to phone for instructions. He need not have worried about my leaving. I was worn out and hurt and didn't think I could go much farther. He came out of the building with a smile on his face. He said he had found a doctor for me. We would just have to walk a little farther. I finally made it to my feet, and we walked to the edge of town and into a large barbed wire enclosure, but one without guard towers.

A young Frenchman guided me to a room crowded with triple bunks spaced closely together, and indicated that an empty lower bunk would be mine. I requested to see a doctor. The Frenchman said that the doctor was somewhere else. Therefore, I was to rest until he came. I collapsed and passed out on the bunk. The next morning, an orderly woke me and said I should come with him, as Doctor Azorin wished to see me. In the space set aside for an examining room, the doctor examined me and informed me that I had a massive hernia but that he would not operate, as he had no anesthesia, and the pain would be too great for me in my condition. In the meantime, he told me that I should rest in a bed in the infirmary, and that his orderly would provide hot water with which to clean myself. He explained that he was the senior officer for fifteen-thousand French forced laborers. One-half worked on nearby farms, and the other half worked in a steel mill. All were assigned tasks by Dr. Azorin to hamper the German war effort.

Each farm worker had a quota of food to steal and bring back to the camp. The steel-mill workers' task was to sabotage the steel-mill products. One method was to take turns urinating on the hot steel-armor plate. This made the armor brittle and weak.

Dr. Azorin then asked me what I most desired in the way of food. What had I missed most from my American diet? After a moment, I mentioned that I had not had a fresh egg since I left America. I wanted not a powdered egg, but a real, fresh egg that had to be cracked open. He said for me to freshen up, and my breakfast would soon be served. His orderly brought me a fried egg, sunny side up, together with toast, jam, and a cup of ersatz coffee. Although the coffee was ersatz, I enjoyed the breakfast!

Doctor Azorin said he had to leave on his rounds and would not be back until evening. He had several French patients at different locations plus most of the soldiers from the 106th Infantry Division who had surrendered and had been treated poorly by the Nazis on the march to the camp. He explained that in the beginning, he had been allowed to use public transportation, but that now he had to ride a bicycle to make his rounds, and it took much time to get to each camp.

I rested during the day and enjoyed a sponge bath when the orderly brought me hot water. That evening I was invited to eat with the doctor, who was clad in pajamas made from a Nazi flag. The swastika was located in a very strategic spot. He would have been shot if the Goons had seen him, but he enjoyed his little joke.

All the while I was in the labor camp, Doctor Azorin was telling the Goons I was dying, while his

orderly was preparing food for me to eat. I had an abscessed tooth bothering me. Doctor Azorin said he would take care of it. I expressed my amazement since he was a medical doctor and not a dentist. He assured me that in France, all medical doctors take care of their patients' teeth. The next day, the orderly brought into the examining room a contraption looking like a one-wheel bicycle with cables attached to it. The doctor entered, sat on the bicycle and, while pumping the bicycle, drilled a hole into my tooth. He then used a tiny corkscrew to insert into and pull out the nerve. The hole was then patched with arsenic and cement. The pain stopped, and the repair lasted until I got home.

I was feeling stronger, and Dr. Azorin got me a truss from somewhere for my hernia. I was able to walk around the buildings and talk to the survivors of the 106th Infantry Division and to listen to their complaints. As the only American officer in camp, I began to collect data for the war trials that I knew were planned.

A surprise inspection by the Goons resulted in their discovery that I was not dying, but in fact, was recovering quite well. I was told to be ready to move within the hour. Oh well, it had been great while it lasted. I'm certain that Doctor Azorin and his orderly saved my life. I was still pretty lucky.

The German officer in charge of the camp was a staunch adherent to the Geneva Convention. Since I was an officer, I should therefore have an orderly. A Serbian enlisted POW was assigned to accompany my guard and me for the trip to an officers' POW camp. This requirement, although correct according to the Geneva Convention, created complications for me. The Germans insisted that the orderly must carry my blanket roll and a small parcel of food provided by Doctor Azorin. As an officer, I must travel with my guard in a second-class compartment of the train, but my orderly, as an enlisted POW, must travel in the baggage car.

After a futile argument to keep my possessions with me, we boarded the train. As the train started to pull out, it suddenly stopped.

A messenger boarded the train with new orders for me to get off this train and rush to another train pulling out soon. Despite my complaints concerning my possessions, the guard escorted me to the second train. There had been no time to get my orderly on the second train. I lost my blanket roll, possessions, and food! I hoped the orderly enjoyed them.

HARASSING THE NAZIS

After the guard and I boarded the second train, he ordered the seated passengers to remove themselves from the second-class compartment. One heavy-set German man put up an argument until the guard shifted his grip on his rifle, ready to strike the objector. After the four civilians left the compartment, the guard motioned for me to enter and be seated. He locked the door, sat down opposite, and stared out the window.

All this time, I had been getting more and more angry at the stupid Goons who had separated me from my blanket and food. I finally had to express my indignation and proceeded to state my opinion of the German authorities who adhered to the Geneva Convention on some minor point but ignored it on major issues. The guard sat staring at me without any expression on his face. Angered by his lack of attention, I embarked on a description of his apparent stupidity and ancestry, using all of the negative words I had ever learned in English, Spanish, and Italian. When I finally ran out of wrath and breath, he very calmly said in perfect English, "War is certainly hell, isn't it, lieutenant." I was astonished and embarrassed by his gentlemanly response to my outburst. Of course, I agreed that war was hell!

The guard continued, saying he understood my anger at losing my possessions and at the lack of coordination by those who changed the orders at the last minute, but he assured me that I wouldn't miss any meals unless circumstances caused us both to miss meals. He revealed that every stop at a station had a soldiers' canteen where we would both eat together. This was something new to me. Soldiers' canteens? Eat with a guard in a room full of enemy soldiers? I didn't want to miss any meals, but how would the enemy soldiers react to a Kriegie eating the same food in the same room with them? Many possibilities occurred to me, not all of them pleasant.

To clarify the situation, I asked him if we

would be in close contact with the German troops. If so, how would they react? The guard assured me that as I was an American officer on my way to a POW camp under guard, and as the war was coming to an end soon, that unless we happened upon a soldier suffering from a psychosis, everything would be all right. The guard said that if we happened to meet an abusive soldier he would protect me. Although I was reassured, I had my doubts. All I could do was wait and see what would happen when we stopped at a station with a soldiers' canteen.

The time came for a test. The train stopped in a fair-sized station, because the tracks ahead of us had been bombed. The guard directed me to leave the train and go into an adjoining building. It was crowded with German soldiers who immediately turned and stared at us. The guard said to take an empty seat at the end of a long plank table. He sat next to me. A large middle-aged woman approached and conversed with my guard. She returned with two bowls of watery soup, two chunks of black bread, and two cups of ersatz coffee. She glared at me, but that didn't spoil my appetite. My manners were not too neat. I dipped the dry bread into my soup to soften it and consumed both before the guard finished eating. I took my time with the coffee and stared back at the Goons who were staring at me. The guard softly asked me not to stare as it might provoke some trouble, which he wouldn't welcome. I thought about his request and decided to go along with it.

The whistle tooted. We boarded, and the guard again cleared the compartment of civilians. He said we should be at the officers' camp before too long if there were no more interruptions to our trip. He said he had never been to the town before, but he had heard there were many camps for different nationalities that had been established for a long time. Therefore, it should be well run with a good supply of necessities and food. I felt encouraged.

We arrived at Hammelberg. The guard said it would be a short walk up the hill to a castle. I had

had those short walks before and didn't believe him. It was a long walk before we reached the castle, and I was subjected to the most complete and humiliating search of my person to date. All clothing—boots, socks, and shorts were removed. Then all bandages and tapes were pulled off. In my condition, it was not pleasant for me nor the person searching me. Unfortunately, the lists of Goons I had prepared at the French labor camp for the war trials were discovered under the tape on my stinking feet. The searcher looked triumphant. The German Commandant Oberst Hoepple asked, "What are these lists?"

I answered, "These are lists of Germans to be tried for violations of the Geneva Convention against the troops of the 106th Infantry Division."

Smiling, and turning to an orderly he commanded, "Burn these lists."

I countered, "Other lists have been prepared, although I don't know where they are by now." And then defiantly, I conjectured, "Maybe your name is on such a list somewhere!"

He told me to get dressed and ordered me to be taken to the dungeon. However, I didn't end up in a dungeon. Instead, I was quartered with a mixed group of POW officers: air corps, tankers, and infantry in the first floor of the castle. Most of the floor was below the ground level, but barred windows were above the grade of the ground outside. I was directed to a bunk and one of the other Kriegies gave me an extra U.S. Army blanket. I sacked out.

The next morning we were issued a cup of coffee and a piece of black bread. I stood looking out of the barred windows at the surrounding area and soon saw a group of POWs walking by with their arms loaded with American Red Cross food parcels. Sam J. Dwyer, Jr., an American tank officer, stood nearby. So I asked him, "Where are the POWs taking the Red Cross food parcels?"

"The POWs are from one of the Slav camps and the food is going to the Slavs, but none of the American Red Cross parcels has ever come into the American POW camp."

He was very upset that all the POW camps were eating American food, but no Americans were getting any.

I asked, "Why aren't the Americans getting any Red Cross parcels?"

"Because the senior American officer is a gutless wonder and is even afraid to talk to the Goons."

I found this hard to believe. All the senior American officers in other camps protected their men by demanding that the rights of the Geneva Convention be observed. Both Gen. Vanaman and Col. Spivey were West Pointers who had always inspired their men with exemplary leadership. The group of officers around me began to express their opinions of our senior officer. They were not complimentary. They insisted that their colonel had led them into an ambush during the Battle of the Bulge, and when the Germans demanded their surrender, he complied even though he had only four minor casualties. He had even refused to let his men spike their weapons or blow up their vehicles, threatening any man disobeying his orders with court martial. The Germans were so delighted with the easy victory that they let the officers of the 106th Infantry Division drive their vehicles to the POW camp at Hammelberg. The GIs of the 106th were not so lucky. They were marched through snowstorms to the French labor camp. I had not believed the stories of the GIs, but something was certainly wrong here.

I decided to find out for myself. I located the colonel's quarters and found that even if his men were short of food and necessities, he and his staff were operating with all the red tape of peacetime assignment. I introduced myself to the adjutant and requested permission to speak to the senior American officer. I next saw the executive officer and made the same request and explained why I wanted to see him. Permission was granted, and I was ushered into the colonel's office. I explained that I had been a Kriegie for over a year, and that I had served under Gen. Vanaman, Col. Spivey, and the French senior officer Dr. Azorin.

I told him that we POWs had rights and were protected under the Geneva Convention, and that all the other senior officers had fought for and protected their men.

Suddenly, the colonel started sobbing with tears running down his cheeks! He stated that he couldn't do anything because the Germans would shoot him, and he wanted to get back to his wife and kiddies. Astounded and shocked, I saw that there was no way to help him, even though his officers assured me that he had been a tough garrison C.O., and that even an unbuttoned pocket brought punishment under his command.

I returned to my bunk trying to decide what to do. Several officers asked me how I made out. I told them, saying that the colonel was not at all typical of other senior officers that I had encountered. I also told them how Kriegies in other camps operated to better themselves and hinder the enemy. They asked me to help organize them along the same lines, as they had no respect for the colonel or some of the other officers who apparently were influenced by his attitude. I agreed, and outlined what had to be done. First, we needed wire cutters, and I explained how to make them from pieces of our bunks. Next, we needed "bitch" committees to call on the German commandant every two hours complaining about violations of rights under the Geneva Convention. We created lots of committees, each consisting of four Krie-gies, so that no one Kriegie or committee could be separated out for punishment. Then, during air raids, we cut through the fences to the German barracks, liberated everything not nailed down, and brought the loot back to our quarters before the Goons came out of the air raid shelters.

Only officers who volunteered took part in the strategy, but all the others got their share too. The plan worked. At last, we had an *esprit de corps* that provided us with food and fuel from broken furniture. Finally the "bitch" committees got the American Red Cross food parcels coming in. Things looked much better for about two weeks, when suddenly a guard came and escorted me up to the German commandant's office. General Gunther Van Goeckel was seated at his desk. Looking up at me, he expressed his displeasure, "Before you arrived here, I had the best behaved POWs in Germany. But since you arrived, my life has become a living hell!"

I saluted and said, "Thank you, sir!"

He replied, "You are going to be out of Hammelberg within the hour!"

And he kept his word! After he gave me two week's lieutenant's salary in Kriegsgefangen marks and made me sign in compliance with Geneva Convention regulations, I was on my way out of Hammelberg.

A CONGENIAL CAPTOR

A different guard, who introduced himself as Max, escorted me from Hammelberg to Nurnberg. He was about my age, slightly built with light brown hair and quiet spoken. As he spoke excellent English, I asked, "How did you learn to speak English so well?"

He replied, "Before the war my family was in the export-import business. I have been in England and America many times as the head of their leather-goods section. I really miss the trips and sightseeing in foreign countries."

"Have any of your military assignments taken you into combat?"

"Yes. My last combat duty was in Italy before my outfit was forced back into Germany by Allied troops."

"You should be glad that the war is almost over because now you can return to your old job in the family business."

With a wry smile he said, "There may not be any family business to return to."

When we arrived at the train station in Hammelburg, I asked, "Max, is there a soldiers' canteen in the station?"

"Yes. Most stations have soldiers' canteens with free food like soup, bread, and coffee, but anything else costs money. Unfortunately, I don't have any money because I always send my pay home to my wife and child. Otherwise, we could enjoy some good German beer with my rations of bread, cheese and sausage."

"Are Kriegsgefangen marks any good for buying beer?"

His eyes lighted up. "Of course, they are good! Do you have any?"

Showing him my money, I suggested, "If you provide the bread, cheese, and sausage, we could use my money to buy beer."

Max agreed. Upon entering the soldiers' canteen, I gave him some money. He left and soon returned with two big mugs of beer. Opening his knapsack, he produced a slab of cheese, a stick of sausage, and half a loaf of bread. We had a feast.

When our train arrived, Max, unlike my previous guard, didn't force all the passengers out of our second class compartment. He only insisted for room for the two of us. He used words, not force. Max seemed like a pretty decent fellow. I thought that maybe he was as tired of the war as I was. As we traveled, I slept until the train's sudden stop woke me up. I asked Max, *"Was ist los?"* He didn't know but inquired of the conductor, who stated that General Patton's troops were on the move again and that they like to shoot up trains. It sounded reasonable to me. The conductor glared but didn't talk to me.

Max commented, "We might be here for some time, so we might as well go into the soldiers' canteen to get something to eat. Perhaps you would like another beer?"

I agreed with this most reasonable German soldier. We enjoyed a repast, washed down with another beer. After some small talk, Max showed me pictures of his wife and child saying, "I'm worried about their safety. I wish they had gone to stay with relatives in the German section of Switzerland."

"Speaking of Switzerland, I always kept the direction of Lake Constance available in case we had to ditch our plane, but unfortunately the plane didn't last long enough to get there. I, too, wish I were in Switzerland. How close to Switzerland does this train go?"

He reached into his pocket and pulled out a small map to illustrate. It looked quite close, and there were railroad tracks that went right into this neutral country. I casually mentioned, "If we should somehow get into Switzerland, it would be worth five hundred dollars in gold to whoever helped me. And besides that, my father would surely match that sum with another five hundred dollars."

Max didn't say anything, but I could see he was thinking about it. He suggested, "Why don't you get some sleep?"

The next morning as we approached Nurnberg, we had the compartment to ourselves. Max locked the door and then quietly told me, "I would like to help you get to Switzerland, but if I do, the SS would certainly shoot my wife and child. I can't take that chance. I know the war is almost over, but my first priority is taking care of my family." As that point settled in, he said, "I've got to go to the restroom and will have to lock you in the compartment, for the conductor is watching us."

As he left, I saw that the small map remained on his seat. I changed my seat, and the map changed owners. I like to think he left the map on purpose. I was pleased to have a map again but disappointed that Max wouldn't or couldn't help me get to Switzerland. I knew it had been a long shot, but I was tired of being a Kriegie. I was down to skin and bones, but in my mind I had kept up a good fight even after being shot down. After seeing how that colonel had crapped out without a fight, I began to wonder why I should keep causing the Goons trouble. Certainly my guards had been fair and had observed the Geneva Convention just as most of the *Wehrmacht* and *Luftwaffe* troops did, but I was getting tired of being cooped up, always hungry, dirty, and tired.

I was depressed. My hopes had been high that Max would go along with my desire to get to Switzerland. My hopes had been too high. Now they hit bottom.

We arrived in Nurnberg at a railroad yard that had really been plastered. Ruins were everywhere, but already the laborers, both men and women, were repairing the damage. We left the station and started walking through the city on the way to the Kriegie camp. The civilians did not look happy. In fact, I have never felt so much hate directed at me as I did that morning in Nurnberg. I was glad to have an armed guard with me. Max set a fast pace through the ruined city and soon we were on the outskirts. I had to slow down. I was tired. It took a lot of effort just to take one step after another. Finally, I told Max that I was through walking. I was tired, and I was going to sit down.

I chose a shady spot under a tree, leaned back against the trunk and said that I was not going to ever move again.

Max implored, "Please lieutenant, please get up. Otherwise, I will have to shoot you."

I pointed to a spot between my eyes and challenged, "Shoot me right there because I'm not getting up or going anywhere!"

He then acquiesced, *"Oh, der krieg ist kaput.* The war is over. I'm not going to shoot you."

He stopped a passing soldier and asked him to contact some authority in the Lager. Soon, I saw a familiar person approaching. It was Popeye Wilhelm Stranghoner, the top noncom from Stalag Luft III where I had been a lifetime ago.

Popeye asked me, "What's the problem?"

I told him, "I am tired. I am hungry. And I am not going to get up and go anywhere."

Popeye asked, "Where did you come from?"

"Hammelberg," I answered.

He shook his head and said, "You are very lucky, because there was a big fight there and many

Kriegies and soldiers were killed."

I didn't believe him, and I didn't move.

"What do you want for getting up and walking into the Lager?" Popeye asked. I refused to answer.

"We have a nice clean barracks that has just been fumigated and some new blankets. Wouldn't that be nice?" he asked. I refused to move or answer.

"You could have a whole Red Cross parcel of food all to yourself," he tempted. I shook my head.

"You can have a nice clean bed in a nice clean barracks with a nice new blanket and a whole Red Cross food parcel to eat. And if you will get up now, you'll be in time for a nice hot shower."

I thought about the hot shower. My last hot shower had been about a year ago.

I asked, "What about soap?"

Popeye replied, "The Red Cross just delivered a boxcar of Swan soap, and you can have a nice, new, still-wrapped bar of Swan soap."

I got up and walked into the Lager. True to his word, Popeye provided me with a hot shower with Swan soap, a Red Cross food parcel, and a new blanket and palliasse in a clean barracks that smelled of sulfur.

Popeye won!

NURNBERG TEDIUM

When I awoke the next morning in Nurnberg, I felt betrayed. I had been naïve. My trust had been misplaced. Believing that a fumigated barracks would have killed any and all pests, I had failed to take the usual precaution of tying strings around my ankles and wrists to keep all creepy, crawly things out. An army of bloodsucking bedbugs had invaded me for the first time! I was angry!

I stripped and commenced killing hundreds of the little bloody bastards. Each of them was engorged with so much of my blood that they could not escape to their hiding places. I squashed them and mashed them, first from my body, then those on my clothes, and finally on my blanket and palliasse. Other Kriegies were doing the same. Apparently, sulfur fumes do not kill bedbugs. After it was dark, they had emerged from the wood of the beds, floors, and walls to gorge on new bodies, especially one that had had over a year's dirt and grime removed by a hot shower. I was angry. The slaughter of bedbugs had taken about three hours, and we had no idea whether we had killed all of them or just their shock troops. We knew to take precautions from then on.

The second shock of the day was to discover that I had been placed in the inner stockade within the larger stockade. The inner stockade was for those who were considered troublemakers or escape artists. The outer area was for those Kriegies who had caused no trouble. Quite a compliment for those of us in the inner compound! We were amazed that the efficient Goons had established the inner compound with so few safeguards. There were areas free from observation that provided safe places to cut through the fences. Of course, with so many Kriegies gathered from all the POW lagers throughout Italy, Austria, France, and Germany, the Goons had been hard pressed to accommodate the many thousands of Kriegies.

We immediately took advantage of the

opportunity. We made some wire cutters and put in place Goon watchers while other Kriegies cut holes in the surrounding barbed-wire fences separating us from the well-behaved Kriegies. I spent about three hours that day wandering through the outer compound looking for friends and acquaintances. Fortunately, I found Ernie McAnulty, a classmate from Hoover High School, class of '38. He had been a big-man-on-campus, a great athlete, but always on the verge of trouble. I wondered how he had escaped being placed in the inner compound. We had a great time bringing each other up-to-date.

I was not surprised that he had not married, since so many girls had competed for his attention for as long as I had known him. Ernie had continued his athletic endeavors in college and had opted for aviation cadets as soon as it was offered. He had completed aviation school, had received his commission, and had been flying a P-38 out of Africa when he was shot down by one of the flak barges placed in the Mediterranean. He had been a Kriegie about twice as long as I had. We parted as an appell was soon coming up.

I had no trouble getting back through the fences into the inner compound. The Kriegie who had cut the fence had done an artistic job in that the cut ends had been bent to hook together. One only had to unhook them to open the entrance and hook them back together afterwards. Only a close examination would reveal the opening. However, after a couple of days, the Goons did discover it. One of the British Colonials, a black soldier, was brought to the opening with tools to repair the fence. Several of us were watching him, but unfortunately no one was watching for Goons. We had thought since the Goons had brought the black soldier and ordered him to repair the fence that there was no need for a Goon-watch. We were wrong. A young German soldier passing by saw several Kriegies watching the black soldier, who was beyond the trip-wire at the fence. The German threw his rifle to his shoulder and shot the British soldier through his head with his first shot. There was no need for a second shot. There was no one else around except the dead British soldier. He was down, and we were gone.

Life went on. Early mornings were times for bedbug slaughter. We broke the tedium by preparing and eating our meager food rations, verbally flying our last missions, planning our futures, cussing the Goons, and cutting new holes in the fences. Artillery and bombs continually broke the silence. One night, the British bombers put on a spectacular display. First, the target markers dropped the flares for the waves of Lancasters coming in with their two-thousand-pound blockbusters to hit Nurnberg. The Goons threw such a concentration of flak into the sky that it seemed impossible for the British to avoid being shot down. The search lights targeting planes, the flares drifting down, the bombs bursting, the flames from the city reaching up to the sky, the noise of the explosions—all of these overwhelmed the senses. Some Kriegies got into slit trenches. I was mesmerized and stood watching the greatest pyrotechnic display I had ever seen, but felt sorry for the crew flying into that holocaust.

It had to happen! One of the Lancasters was in difficulty and veered from its course over Nurnberg and headed toward us. It salvored its bombs as the plane burst into flame. We could hear the sound of the bomb approaching, and everyone hit the ground. The bomb exploded about a block from our Lager. The blast moved the barracks about six feet. No one was seriously hurt since there was no glass in the windows to shatter. However, the bomb blast silenced the camp for me. Both eardrums were ruptured again. I could hear nothing for several days.

Life continued. The routine slowed down for me. I was learning to lip-read until my hearing returned. The lack of hearing made me cautious. I waited and watched until I was beginning to hear some sounds. Fellow Kriegies informed me that General Patton's armies were approaching. I hoped he wouldn't screw up like he had at Hammelberg. Soon, we were told to get ready to move out.

At last, being classed as a troublemaker paid off. The troublemakers got a 40-and-8-boxcar trip to Moosburg. All others had to walk.

THE LAST BIG BATTLE

As the sound of artillery came closer to Nurnberg, the rumors multiplied. The most persistent rumor was that the Kriegies would be removed to a redoubt in the Alps, an area where we would be held and used as a bargaining chip to ensure safe treatment for Hitler and his friends. This area would be defended by rabid SS troops who would liquidate all POWs if the bargaining failed. Since we troublemakers were the first to be removed from Nurnberg and honored by being the only group to be moved by train, this rumor gained strength.

We devised many plans to escape. Some were logical, but most were harebrained. Since the Good Lord had helped me avoid death so far, and I now weighed only sixty-five pounds and was too weak to do much, I made no plans.

The 40-and-8 boxcars were even more crowded than usual, but we had the advantage of seeing U.S. warplanes escorting our train. As the planes flew by, the pilots dipped their wings to let us know that they knew it was a POW train, not an enemy train. When we arrived in Moosburg, a small town about twenty kilometers north, northeast of Munich, we were marched into the biggest Lager I had ever seen. Over a hundred thousand POWs of all nationalities were located in and around Moosburg. We troublemakers again were marched into an inner camp within a larger camp. We had the advantage of being placed in barracks similar to those in Stalag Luft III, except that here, each housed about 400 POWs, more than three times as many as at the camp at Sagan. We were in a building, whereas most of the Kriegies were packed beneath large tents. Even the tents were inadequate, and thousands slept in the open until some crude shelters were constructed. Some areas looked like a village for homeless refugees, except that all were enclosed by barbed wire.

The Kriegie population of Moosburg consisted of French, British, Serbian, Italian,

American, and Russian POWs, with the poor Russians being the most abused. Water was obtained from a few faucets or hand pumps that required a long wait in line just to fill a klim can. Sanitation was practically non-existent. Disease under such conditions was widespread, and POW doctors had few means to minister to the sick and dying.

The few elderly guards were unable or unwilling to keep Kriegies under strict control. They knew that their *"krieg ist kaput!"* The senior German officers were friendlier and were amenable to the senior American officers' suggestions to get more food into camp. We heard that an agreement was reached that allowed a convoy of trucks, under YMCA protection, to bring tons of food parcels from Switzerland to Moosburg. It must have been true since we were each issued one-half of a Red Cross food parcel per week—not enough to gain weight but enough to survive.

Again, I went through the fence and found Ernie McAnulty in one of the tents. I suggested that he might like to join the troublemakers and move into our barracks, since some of the more recent Kriegies had already escaped the camp and there was now room for Ernie. He joined us, and we discussed plans for our action after liberation. We both were upset with some of the Goons who had been too liberal with their gun butts and decided to locate and to punish them. We also agreed that we were never going to be hungry again and would use any means possible to avoid being hungry. Being warm at all times was another priority, as was unrestricted freedom of movement. Our priorities being set, we awaited liberation.

The sound of battle grew louder. We saw armored vehicles approaching and thought we were liberated. We were wrong. It was an SS group. The Goons took one of our senior officers to the front between the armies for pending negotiations. When arrangements broke down, they brought him back to camp. Word soon passed throughout the camp that we should dig more slit trenches, as the area around the camp would come under attack the next morning.

Sunday, April 29, 1945, was a day to remember. Explosions were so heavy and so close that the ground trembled. Soon the sky was full of P-47s and P-51s, strafing and dive-bombing. The sound of tanks and artillery grew louder, and Piper Cubs flew over, observing the artillery fire. They looked so small and weak compared to the P-47s and P-51s—like dragonflies surrounded by hawks and eagles. As bullets and flak began falling into the camp, we got into the slit trenches for protection. I hated to miss seeing the action. Therefore, every so often I would pop my head up to see what was going on. I got lucky! I saw one of the guards in a tower firing his machine gun at a P-51. The pilot did a chandelle and a 180-degree turn. He came back with all guns firing, blowing the tower into kindling. But American senior officers were running around ordering us to keep down for our safety. I followed orders and kept my head down, even though I hated to miss the show. We heard that some Kriegies were killed. What a waste, with liberation so close.

The sound of battle reached a crescendo! Then suddenly, silence. The firing had stopped. It was hard to believe! Ernie and I jumped out of our trench and ran to the entrance of the camp to watch for our troops. An American tank approached followed by a bunch of GIs and a jeep with some joker in a chromium-plated helmet as a passenger. He must have had a death wish! One of the Goon guards in a tower started shooting a rifle. We ducked and watched as the tank's 75mm cannon moved to aim at the tower. One blast, no tower! All was peaceful for a moment, and then a roar of celebration arose from the masses of Kriegies.

The joker in the fancy helmet stood up and waved. It was General Patton. An American flag was run up the flagpole. For us the war should have been over.

FAREWELL TO WAR

The thousands of ex-POWs went crazy! Some were shouting and cheering; others were crying! As soon as the Red Cross started up the donut machines, some ex-Kriegies started eating donuts like there was no tomorrow. For some, there would be no tomorrow. Unfortunately, most of us had shrunken digestive tracts from the starvation diet, and the mass of hot donuts ruptured their stomachs. Many died on their first day of liberation with the help of Red Cross donuts. The army doctors stopped the donut machines and brought in some soft-ice-cream machines.

Ernie and I wanted to get outside the barbed wire fences, and we did. At the first farmhouse we encountered, we liberated a couple of bicycles and rode farther from the camp. We came to a large, well-kept, two-story farmhouse with neat outbuildings. We stopped and knocked on the door. When no one came to the door, we entered. The house appeared to be deserted. Leaving an empty kitchen, we went downstairs into a basement and found a treasure trove of food. There were bins of turnips, potatoes, and cabbages. Smoked hams and sausages hung from the beams.

Suddenly, we heard footsteps on the stairs. Soon a short, stout German entered the basement. He welcomed us and inquired as to what we desired. We answered that we were hungry and for him to get his wife down to cook some food. He asked us not to hurt his wife or daughter. We replied that all we wanted was some food, but we wanted it quickly! I asked him if he were a Nazi. He appeared shocked at the idea. However, when I dug into the potato bin and found a uniform belt and a small jeweled dagger wrapped in a Nazi flag, he admitted that most good Germans had to pretend to be Nazis.

His wife prepared sliced ham and fried potatoes. After eating, we rode back to camp to see what changes had been made. As we approached camp, we decided that we had better find a place to hide our liberated bicycles so that they would not be stolen. We stacked them in a ravine and covered them with brush. Leaving the bikes well hidden, we entered camp and were soon brought up to date. Many American ex-POWs had gone into Moosburg and liberated booze and food. The Serb ex-POWs had stayed in their Lager like well-behaved Kriegies. The poor Russian ex-POWs had left camp and were raising all kinds of hell. They had gotten guns from somewhere and were killing and raping. After the way the Germans abused them, I was not surprised. However, they had caused so much havoc that American GIs had to round them up and put them back into camp where GIs in the guard towers could keep the Russians under control. The Russians were prisoners again. They were told that they would be kept in camp until Russian authorities came to escort them back to Russia. This news caused mass suicide among them. It was difficult for me to understand their preference for death over going home.

The army told us Americans that we were to stay in camp, be good, and wait in an orderly way to be documented before being flown home in a couple of weeks. In the meantime, we would be deloused and fed. Ernie and I talked about the orders and decided to ride our bikes along with the troops as the front line moved. We bashed that night and left camp the next morning. It was easy, as GI sentries were not as alert as German sentries.

When we got to the ravine where we had hidden our bikes, we got a shock! Some thief had stolen our liberated bicycles! We couldn't keep up with the front line on foot. We needed transportation. After a short walk toward town, we found a garage. Forcing entry, we were delighted to find a German staff car. This was a six-wheeled Mercedes touring sedan with flags on the front fenders, the key in the ignition switch, and a box of hand grenades in the back seat. We took the flags off the fenders and liberated the Mercedes. The gas tank was full as we took off to catch up with the U.S. Army.

Photo Courtesy Daimler Chrysler

Along the way, we saw a graceful chalet close by a small tranquil lake. I asked Ernie if he would like to eat some fish. He was agreeable. We drove by the chalet out where a stream splashed a thin waterfall over a dam. I pulled the pin on a grenade and threw it into the lake. A geyser of water erupted, and fish began to float to the surface. Suddenly, a German came running and shouting. I pulled the pin on another grenade and waited for him. He finally explained that he was the dam keeper and was afraid the explosions would damage the wooden gates of the dam and cause a flood down the valley. We accepted his explanation. I put the pin back into the grenade and ordered him to lie down by the spillway to catch the fish for our next meal. When he collected enough, we told him to clean and cook them for us.

We went with him into the chalet where his wife finished cleaning and preparing the fish for us. While the meal was being cooked, I went on a tour of the basement and again found uniforms, daggers, medals, and Nazi flags in the potato bin. What was the idea of hiding everything in potato bins? Some Nazi S.O.P? When I asked the dam keeper about the uniform, he denied knowing anything about it, as he had never been a Nazi!

After a good meal washed down with beer, we decided that there was no reason to return to our camp near Moosburg where some thief might steal our liberated Mercedes. We drove down from the lake and onto a road that looked like it had had a lot of use. Suddenly, a Messerschmitt fighter plane came toward us from out of the blue. We expected to be strafed, but apparently the pilot saw the German Iron Cross painted on the Mercedes and flew off looking for enemies.

Over a few more hills and down a valley, we saw a large U.S. Army encampment and decided to make a cautious approach to see if we could fill up our gas tank. We caused a lot of excitement and were soon surrounded by many GIs and a few officers, one of whom looked familiar. I stood up and asked if there were anyone from San Diego. The familiar-looking officer rapidly approached our Mercedes. He was Major Ray Fellows, supply officer for the 5th Corps, whom I had known at San Diego State College. We briefed him about our experiences, telling him where we had been and what we were doing. He asked if there were anything he could do for us. We suggested that we were always hungry and would appreciate it if he could help us out with some food. Asking what we would like, we responded with, "How about a small steak and a bottle of red wine about every two hours?"

He replied, "No problem. What else can I do for you?"

Jokingly, I asked, "Do you have any fur-lined fatigues?"

After thinking for a moment, Ray said, "I don't have any on hand, but by 4:00 P.M., I will have some. In the meantime, you can eat, get cleaned up, and rest while I have your Mercedes serviced and secured until you are ready to leave."

That sounded good to us!

His supply sergeant liberated some furs and sewed them inside new fatigues, and by 4:00 P.M. we were fed, cleaned up and wearing fur-lined fatigues. We stayed with Ray and enjoyed his hospitality of small steaks and red wine for five days. I gained fifteen pounds.

When we left Ray, we decided not to go to war again but to start on the road home.

15

HELLO PARIS!

ack on the road again, we headed north-west in our Mercedes. We didn't have any maps but didn't need them because the only signs we saw read, *"Achtung Minen,"* which we interpreted as, "Attention, these roads are loaded with land mines." We didn't have any mine-detection equipment and doubted that we would have used any if we had had it.

Suddenly, I finally realized that I was no longer a Kriegie. I was totally free! I knew I had a future! Tears came to my eyes. I couldn't stop them. I hadn't cried like this since I was a kid when the doctor straightened and stretched my polio-damaged leg before putting on a new cast. Ernie brought me back to the present by asking me if I had any suggestions as to how to get to Le Havre and Camp Lucky Strike, the staging area for GIs returning home. I told him to keep going west-northwest as fast as possible, so if any land mines exploded, they would blow up behind us. Ernie agreed and put the pedal to the metal. Fortunately, no land mines exploded.

The Mercedes was a magnificent automobile, powerful and comfortable. In fact, this was the most comfortable transportation either of us had had since landing in the Third Reich. The only problem was the high rate of consumption of gasoline as we roared over the deserted roads. We stopped to fill up the tanks whenever we saw a military encampment. However, the farther we traveled away from the fighting front, the more difficult it was to obtain gasoline and a friendly offer of food. We got both at each stop, but it took more persuasive arguments and wasted our time.

Presently, we were both aware that we were no longer just survivors with no past nor future. We not only had the now, the immediate present, but we had a future, and we became most demanding toward these non-combatants who had cushy jobs far behind the front lines.

We stopped that night with a P-51 fighter

group that had recently arrived in Germany from the States. The pilots were most friendly and had many questions concerning conditions at the front and about how each of us had been shot down. During the evening, we mentioned that obtaining gasoline for our Mercedes was getting more difficult the farther we got from the front. The squadron C.O. had a suggestion for us. He had a Citroën painted OD color with forged papers and plates. It got excellent miles-per-gallon, and he was willing to trade us his Citroën for our Mercedes. His squadron had unlimited gasoline, and with forged papers and plates, we would have no trouble filling up at any fuel dump in occupied Europe. We traded.

The Citroën wasn't as pretty a car. In fact, it looked as though it sagged in the middle, but the greater miles per gallon was more important than beauty. Pretty is as pretty does, and the forged papers and plates helped too. We took off in our Citroën the next morning and had no difficulty obtaining gasoline and oil at each fuel dump.

What really amazed us was the excellent mileage the little car got and also how rapidly we were approaching Paris—assuming the mileage signs were correct.

We decided that our tour of Germany and Austria had covered enough sights and sounds, and that all young Americans should visit Paris before returning home. We each had a small suitcase of souvenirs from our Germanic travels and believed we should have some presents for our families from France. We continued heading west-northwest, and the Citroën seemed to run even better, just like a horse going home to its stable. There was not much traffic on the roads, and we made excellent progress. Soon we were approaching the outskirts of Paris. The closer we got to the city, the more people we encountered, and soon we were driving at a crawl because of the crowds.

There seemed to be some kind of civil disturbance. We heard gunshots and saw angry crowds pushing and shoving young women around. There were even groups of people shaving the heads of the young women. I told Ernie we had better get off the streets and get our Citroën into a locked garage before these people got wilder.

We saw a French policeman, and Ernie, who knew some French, asked for directions to a garage. The policeman spoke English and offered to show us to his brother's hotel that had garages to rent. After we had the car safely locked away, I breathed a sigh of relief. I hadn't expected the French people to be so angry. I could still hear gunshots being fired and was apprehensive of people who would abuse young women and even shave off their hair. I spoke to the policeman of my concerns. He laughed and said,

"Oh, don't worry, my friend. My people will love and protect you. We are just celebrating the end of the war and getting even with collaborators. The Boche has surrendered! Hitler is dead! This is a victory celebration, and without you Americans, it wouldn't have happened!"

Ernie and I knew that for us, the war had ended when General Patton liberated our prison camp, but we had no idea that the war was over. We decided that we should check with the U.S. Army Headquarters and send messages home to our families. We asked directions from the policeman and started walking. We were immediately surrounded by crowds and offered bottles of wine and so many handshakes, kisses, and pats on the back that we had difficulty walking.

Since I was unable to converse in French, I had to depend on Ernie to translate for me. One particularly aggressive young woman would not let go of me. She got nose to nose with me and said, *"Oh, le pauvre prisonnier de guerre affamé! Venez avec moi,"* and on and on for about five minutes. I asked Ernie what she was saying.

He said, "I think she wants to take you home with her and make a pet out of you."

"Tell her thanks," I replied, "but no thanks because I am married, and all I want right how is a hot shower, clean clothes, and some American food."

We continued to walk and finally reached

the U.S. Headquarters, where we were deloused with DDT, had hot showers, and were issued new uniforms. Dinner was roast beef, mashed potatoes, wrinkled peas, and apple pie-a-la-mode—an old-fashioned American meal. We were assigned to quarters and went to bed but couldn't sleep because of the food and the sound of sentries' footsteps protecting us from the enemy.

But who and where were the enemy?

When Surrender Was Not An Option

16

SEEING THE SIGHTS

Neither Ernie nor I slept well that night. The next morning we had a typical American breakfast of ham, eggs, potatoes, toast, and real coffee. After breakfast, we were told it was possible to draw $400 against our back salary. We each drew the maximum and received strange, colorful, tissue thin currency instead of greenbacks.

We left the military headquarters to see Paris. The Louvre was all boarded up, but at the Eiffel Tower, we were allowed to climb part way up to get a view of the city. However, what was most exciting for me was to go down to the Metro station and ride the trains. This was the first subway I had ever seen, and I was amazed at how well it was engineered, constructed, and thoughtfully designed. From a commuter's standpoint, the whole system worked. We rode for a few hours with a most friendly population who made certain that we were not lost and guided us back to our hotel where our Citroën was garaged.

When we entered the hotel, we were warmly welcomed and assured that our automobile was safe and secure. We asked at the desk where we could buy Chanel No. 5—the only French perfume we had ever heard of—to take home to our families. Our question triggered a volatile conversation among some of the hotel residents and employees as to the best and least expensive place to shop. The conclusion was that we should go to the factory to ensure that we would obtain the real Chanel No. 5 and not some imitation.

Receiving our directions, we set out for the factory. To walk the streets with no barbed wire in sight was a pleasure. We could see, however, the many bullet scars on the buildings, which told us of the firefights that had taken place.

At the perfume factory, we encountered other ex-Kriegies who had returned to Paris after experiencing chaos and confusion at Camp Lucky Strike. They explained that there was an apparent shortage of food because the food stockpiled for the ex-POWs had been sold on the French Black Market by members of the U.S. Supply Corps. Each day was spent lining up for breakfast, immediately lining up for lunch, followed by immediately lining up for dinner. If an ex-POW didn't get into a chow-line soon enough, he had to go hungry. Since there was no shortage of food at headquarters in Paris, we were skeptical that food could be in such short supply. We decided that we would check out this information before committing ourselves to Camp Lucky Strike. Since the sergeant at the U.S. Head-quarters had suggested that we sign up for trans-portation to the camp, we decided not to go back to headquarters but to try to rent a room at the hotel where our Citroën was garaged.

After making our purchases of perfume, we wandered back to the hotel, marveling at the scen-ery. We were shocked by men relieving themselves in public *pissoirs*, while tipping their *chapeaus* to ladies passing by. However, we were happy to be free to wander and observe the passing scene.

At the hotel, we were again welcomed and shown rooms on the second and third floors reached by stairs too narrow for people to pass each other. The minuscule rooms were approximately eight by six feet with a water closet. Each room had a narrow bed, a cold water basin, a very small table, and one chair. There was no closet, but there were hooks on the wall for clothes. We decided to rent separate rooms so we wouldn't be cramped.

Our inquiry about a restaurant again caused a noisy discussion before a consensus was reached. Our advisors directed us to an address that would not look like a restaurant, but merely a door on the street where we were told to knock and ask for Maurice. The hotel manager said he would phone ahead and make arrangements. We did as directed, knocked, and asked for Maurice. The restaurant was quite large, consisting of many small rooms, with a nicely furnished courtyard and a sec-ond-floor balcony. The courtyard tables had table-cloths and subdued lighting from small lamps that created a comfortable, relaxed ambiance. Coming through the rather shabby door on the street into this luxurious oasis was quite a surprise. Maurice appeared and introduced himself, welcomed us, and said that most Parisians did not dine until after 10:00 P.M. Since we were early, we could have anything on the menu, as he knew we had been *prisonniers de guerre*. The dinner was delicious even though everything seemed to have sauce on it. However, the ever-full glass of wine cleansed the palate quite well. The dinner was even more enjoyable since there was no charge. We were guests of the management.

We returned to the hotel and managed to sleep. In the morning, the manager requested us to have breakfast before we left for the day. To our surprise, it was real coffee and a delicious, fresh-baked roll. We thanked the manager and told him that we would not be back until quite late, as we were going to Le Havre to reconnoiter Camp Lucky Strike.

We took the Metro as far as we could to

the outskirts of Paris and then walked some distance before starting to hitchhike. We were lucky.
A large Cadillac limousine with OD paint and U.S.
markings stopped. The driver, a sergeant, asked
where we were heading. We said we were going
to Camp Lucky Strike, and he invited us to ride
in the back on the jump seats. To our surprise a
WAC second lieutenant sat in the back seat holding a small Scottish terrier. After introducing ourselves, Ernie asked, "How do you rate a Caddy and
a chauffeur?"

Laughing, she replied, "I'm not the one
who rates a Caddy. It's the young Scottie. I just
came along to keep the dog company. He is a son
of President Roosevelt's dog Fala, and is a gift from
the president to General Eisenhower."

This probably was the closest I would ever
come to royalty. The Scottie and his two servants
dropped us off near the camp. We entered to find
that our previous information about the treatment
of the ex-POWs had not been exaggerated. Long
lines of ex-POWs extended everywhere. We talked

to some of our friends and discovered that Camp Lucky Strike was a SNAFU. There was no chance of a speedy return to the good old USA. We left and hitchhiked back to Paris.

When Surrender Was Not An Option

GOING HOME

When Ernie and I arrived in Paris, we decided to check out the Officers' Club. We had heard that they served great hors d'oeuvres in the bar. After seeing how the army was treating ex-POWs at Camp Lucky Strike, we wanted to compare it to the everyday life of the ground pounders and pencil pushers at headquarters. We were not disappointed. One could pick out Headquarters Staff Officers by the bevy of Red Cross girls they were escorting. None of them seemed to be suffering.

While we were drinking a beer, four flying officers came over and sat at our table. They had just arrived from the States and landed their B-17 bomber at Orly Airport and were spending the night in Paris before flying down to the French Riviera in the morning. When they began questioning us about Paris, we explained that we had just arrived a few days before from Germany and were not experts on life in Paris. When they heard that we were ex-POWs, they bought us more beer and wanted to know how each of us had been shot down. They expressed disappointment that they had arrived too late to fly any combat missions. We disabused them of that idea and told them that they might have a chance to fly missions against Japan or Russia. It still bothered us that the Russian POWs, despite their abusive treatment from the Goons, had preferred death to returning to Mother Russia. It couldn't be a very civilized country if Russian POWs preferred self-strangulation to a return home.

The crew insisted on taking us out to dinner. Although we were always hungry, we couldn't compete with our hosts when it came to putting away food. Our stomachs were still shrunken. During the meal, their first pilot suggested that we meet at Orly Field in the morning and fly down to the Riviera. It sounded like a good idea. We told them we would see them in the morning and returned to our hotel.

The next day, we got up early, had a cup of coffee with the manager, and took the Metro out to Orly. We located their plane and placed our bags of liberated souvenirs inside, as none of the crew had arrived. I suggested that they might be in the mess hall having breakfast. We went in but did not find them there. We decided to have another coffee and roll while we waited for them.

Finally, we went back out on the field just in time to see the B-17 taking off with our bags on board. Alarmed, we ran to the tower and requested the operations officer to radio them and order them to return to base. There was no reply even though they were required to monitor that wavelength. After several attempts to contact them, the operations officer offered to have the MPs meet them when they landed to recover our bags. It was obvious that the crew had stolen our bags of Germanic souvenirs. As a new crew just over from the states, the temptation to obtain Nazi paraphernalia was too great to resist. We declined his offer. These were just the wages of war.

On our way back to Paris, I told Ernie that maybe this misfortune was a sign for us to get busy and get on home. He agreed but didn't want to spend two weeks at Camp Lucky Strike. I didn't either, but I had an idea I wanted to try out. My idea was that if some of the officers at Camp Lucky Strike were so crooked as to sell the ex-POWs' rations on the black market, we could use their greed to quickly get on a ship home.

Back at our hotel in Paris, we paid our bills for the garage and rooms and bid a fond farewell to our new friends who had been so caring. Our automobile was gassed up, and we drove to Le Havre. I left Ernie to protect our Citroën, walked into headquarters, and located the officer in charge of cutting orders for a trip to the states. He was a second lieutenant in charge of Squad F Troops who were processing the ex-POWs flying personnel for a return to the USA.

I queried the second lieutenant, "How long will it be before my friend and I will be on orders to ship home?"

He replied, "About two weeks."

I demurred. "That's really too bad."

"Why is that too bad?"

"Well, we have a fine Citroën painted with OD with papers and license plates. When we leave the camp and board a ship, we will have to give the car to someone who has done us a great favor."

Mulling it over, he asked, "Would getting on a ship today be a great favor, and could I see the Citroën?"

"Affirmative to both questions."

After viewing the car, he asked each of us for our full names and serial numbers. Then he instructed, "Wait right here until I get back."

In a few minutes, he returned and handed each of us our orders. We were numbers one and two to board a ship leaving Le Havre that day. We gave him the keys to the car, thanked him, and started walking toward the dock where a new navy hospital ship was loading.

Suddenly, we heard sirens, and looking back saw MP cars with flashing red lights headed toward the Citroën. The MPs stopped there and talked to the second lieutenant who motioned toward us. They then drove to where we were standing. A captain got out and barked, "You men are in big trouble!"

I inquired, "How are we in big trouble?"

He replied, "There's an all-points bulletin about you for obtaining fuel for purposes other than military use."

I countered, "We are not in any trouble. Don't you know about Gen. Eisenhower's order that no ex-POWs are responsible for any crimes committed except rape or murder?"

"Oh, you know about that order?"

"Yes, we do," I assured him.

"Well, I'm still going to impound your car," he threatened.

Ernie and I innocently looked at each other as I stated, "We don't have a car."

"That Citroën is going to be impounded!"

"Go ahead. It's not our Citroën."

"Whose is it?"

"It's his car," I insisted, as I pointed to the second lieutenant standing by the Citroën.

Ernie and I left and boarded the navy hospital ship for a pleasant trip to New York Harbor. We could not have been treated more kindly by the crew who gave us neat, clean bunks, hot showers, food cooked to order, and calm seas all the way.

When we entered the New York Harbor, a flotilla of ships blowing horns and sirens greeted us. Fireboats washed the skies with geysers of water. Then, seeing the Statue of Liberty, we knew we were finally back on home ground.

George Crawford back home

Glossary

abort	to quit; also a German toilet
appell	roll call formation
bash or bashed	to eat greedily
bitch	to complain
chandelle	an abrupt, climbing turn
chapeau	French hat
ditch	to land a plane in water
88s	8.8cm *Flieger Abwehr Kanone* 18, Flying Defense Cannon, or Air Defense Gun
flak	metal from exploding shells
Goon	German soldier
G.P. bombs	general-purpose bombs
horizontal stabilizer	fixed member of a plane's tail
kaput	finished
klim	powdered milk; milk spelled backwards
Kriegie	short version of *Kriegsgefangenen*; an American POW of the Nazis
lager	building, or enclosure

Luftwaffe	German air force
Mae West	inflatable life vest
milk run	no problems; no opposition
N.C.O.	non-commissioned officer
O.D.	olive drab color
pissoirs	French public urinal in the street; covers a man from knees to chest
POW	prisoner of war
prisonniers de guerre	prisoners of war
SS	*Schutzstaffel;* elite Nazi police force
sacked out	to sleep
S.O.P.	standard operating procedure
SNAFU	situation normal, all fouled up
spike	to render a weapon useless
trip wire	boundary; to pass was to get shot
vorlager	camp buildings: Germans' barracks, infirmary, hospital, food & clothing; used as a receiving and processing area for new prisoners

ABOUT THE AUTHORS

George G. Crawford served as a bombardier in the Army Air Corps during World War II. His dramatic military career was played out in Europe until he was liberated by General George Patton.

Following military service, George returned to California where he completed his education and obtained a degree in law in 1962. He has had a long and distinguished career in law from attorney to prosecutor to judge.

George and his wife Esther currently live in his hometown of San Diego, where they are enjoying retirement.

ABOUT THE AUTHORS

James V. Lee retired from Central Texas College as a writing instructor to become an author and publisher. He is the author of *Nine Years In The Saddle* and continues to write and edit other books of timeless historical value.